WHEN THE CITY SHAKES

WHEN THE CITY SHAKES

PREPARING YOURSELF FOR CIVIL UNREST

BARRETT COLE

*To the men and women who do the work
to keep the world from falling off the cliff.*

Table of Contents

Introduction:
Why You're Worried & Why You're Right

As I stepped off the plane in Khartoum in late 2019, the city felt tense, like a coiled spring ready to snap. The Sudanese capital was teetering on the brink of revolution, and you could sense it everywhere: the muted conversations in cafés, the furtive glances exchanged in crowded streets, the unease in the air when groups gathered. I wasn't there as a tourist—I'd traveled for work, unrelated to the current upheaval in the country, but my background as an Intelligence Officer often brought me to places where stability was in short supply. In this instance, that place happened to be at the headwaters of the Nile. Sudan had been simmering for months, with protests against President Omar al-Bashir's regime growing louder, more frequent, and more intense.

I had seen this before in other countries during my travels, but there was something different about this moment. The city was unpredictable, and that made it dangerous. The man walking down the street one minute could quickly see you as an acceptable target to vent his anger and frustration. Traversing the streets required more than just basic planning; it demanded constant situational awareness, a deep understanding of human behavior, and above all, the ability to stay calm in the face of uncertainty.

On that particular trip, I needed to move between meetings, across a city where a protest might flare up at any moment, where police could set up a roadblock or militias could appear seemingly out of nowhere and neither could be trusted to provide protection. I relied on instincts honed over years of experience, knowing that the smallest misstep in a situation like this could be catastrophic. I had to read the crowd, study the street, know when to blend in and when to move quickly.

That evening, I made it back to the hotel just as a large protest erupted in the center of the city. I could hear the distant shouts, and eventually, the sharp crack of gunfire. The city had reached its tipping point. I stayed in place, reviewing my plans for contingencies—ways to get out if the violence moved closer to my location. The US Embassy's number was on speed dial though, at that point, there was little they would be able to do for me. Luckily, I didn't have to act on any of those contingencies, but I knew from long experience the importance of preparation.

I share this story not to frighten you, but to demonstrate that what you may be feeling right now—an unease about the direction things are headed, a fear that instability is growing—is not unwarranted. Civil unrest can happen suddenly, and when it does, being unprepared can put you and your loved ones at unnecessary risk.

I've spent more than a decade navigating some of the world's most unstable places, often arriving in the midst of political or social crises, where unrest wasn't just a possibility—it was reality. I've seen how quickly things can change, how cities can go from calm to chaos in a matter of hours. I've worked in environments where understanding human behavior, situational awareness, and strategic planning were not optional; they were essential to survival.

You don't need to have a military background, combat experience, or an intelligence officer's training like me to prepare for the kinds of risks we face in the modern world. What you need is practical, no-nonsense advice—something that gives you the tools to make rational, informed decisions under stress. That's what this book is about.

You may be reading this because the political climate has you worried, or perhaps recent events have made you question how prepared you really are. Maybe you've started thinking about what would happen if protests or riots broke out in your city, or if social unrest made it unsafe to move freely. These are valid concerns, and I'm here to reassure you that you can take practical steps to protect yourself and your family without succumbing to panic.

This book is designed for people like you—urban and suburban dwellers who may not have military training, who haven't considered themselves "preppers," but who recognize that the world feels more unstable now than it ever has in our lifetime. You don't have to transform into a survival expert overnight. You just need to understand the basics, have a plan, and remain calm. Together, we'll walk through those steps so that no matter what happens, you'll be ready to face it.

The Current Political and Social Climate

In recent years, it's been impossible to ignore the growing sense of instability. You turn on the news, and it feels like society is unraveling in slow motion. Headlines about protests, riots, political violence, and clashes between groups of citizens fill the airwaves. Social media, once a place for connection, now often feels like a battlefield where opposing sides hurl accusations and threats. It's no wonder that you might feel uneasy. These tensions are real, and they're growing.

We live in a time when major events—a contested election, a divisive Supreme Court ruling, or even the fallout from a viral video—can spark unrest. And once unrest begins, it can spread rapidly. What starts as a peaceful protest in one part of a city can quickly turn into something more dangerous as anger boils over and frustration builds. With the political climate as polarized as it is today, many cities have seen periods of unrest, and it doesn't take much for a situation to spiral out of control.

The social contract that keeps everyday life running smoothly—people generally following the rules, respecting boundaries, and cooperating for the greater good—can break down when trust in institutions erodes. Many people today are deeply suspicious of the government, the media, and even law enforcement. As trust weakens, so does the glue that holds society together, making it more vulnerable to flare-ups of violence and chaos.

If you've been feeling a growing sense of dread, you're not alone. The world feels more volatile now than it has in a long time, and it's natural to worry about what comes next. But there's a difference between feeling anxious about the future and allowing fear to paralyze you. While the risks are real, they don't have to control your life. The key is understanding the situation and knowing how to respond rationally if things go wrong.

Civil unrest is not some distant, abstract problem that happens only in foreign countries. In recent years, many of the world's most stable nations have experienced periods of significant turmoil, and the United States is no exception. You may have witnessed protests in your own city or seen footage of buildings burning, people clashing in the streets, or entire neighborhoods being shut down. These events can leave anyone feeling vulnerable, especially if you've never had to think about survival in a crisis before.

It's also important to understand that unrest doesn't have to be widespread to impact you. It doesn't take a nationwide breakdown to make you feel unsafe. Even localized disruptions—whether it's in your neighborhood or a few blocks from your office—can have a profound effect on your life. Roads can be blocked, services disrupted, stores looted. You might find yourself suddenly cut off from resources or unable to move around as freely as you're used to.

These are unsettling possibilities, but they're not reasons to panic. In fact, panic is exactly what you want to avoid. The most important thing you can do is approach the situation with a calm, practical mindset. If you know what to look for, how to plan, and how to react, you can protect yourself and your family from the worst-case scenarios. You don't have to be an expert in survival to make smart decisions in tough situations. You just need a framework—a set of tools that you can rely on when the time comes.

Why It's Normal to Be Worried

It's easy to feel overwhelmed when the world seems to be spinning out of control. After all, if you've lived most of your life without having to think about survival, the thought of facing real danger can be frightening. But here's the truth: feeling worried is a sign that you're paying attention, that you're aware of the world around you. And that's a good thing.

The way we consume media today plays a significant role in amplifying that worry. We are constantly plugged into a steady stream of news, updates, and social media posts that make it feel like every event is happening right in front of us, even if it's hundreds or thousands of miles away. This constant flow of information is new. In previous generations, people learned about major events by reading the morning newspaper or catching the evening news. Today, we have 24/7 access to breaking news, live streams of protests, and real-time updates from people on the ground in moments of crisis. While this access gives us more information than ever before, it also means that we're constantly exposed to the world's most frightening and volatile moments.

Psychologically, this stream of alarming content can make the world seem more dangerous than it actually is. News outlets, social media platforms, and even our own smartphones are designed to keep our attention, and fear is a powerful motivator. Stories about unrest, violence, and political upheaval grab our attention more than positive news because our brains are wired to prioritize potential threats. This "negativity bias" is a survival instinct—a way our ancestors stayed alert to dangers in their environment. In today's media-driven world, that instinct hasn't changed, but the volume of information has skyrocketed.

Every alert, notification, or video we see serves as a reminder that something bad is happening somewhere, and our brains react by heightening our sense of fear and anxiety. Even if these events are happening far away, the immediacy of the images and the tone of the news can make them feel like they're happening right outside our door. We are no longer insulated by distance or time; we experience crises as they unfold, sometimes without all the facts or context, which only increases our sense of vulnerability.

Social media adds another layer of complexity.

Platforms like X, Facebook, and Instagram are filled with personal accounts, opinions, and images that can paint an even more chaotic picture than traditional news outlets. We see videos of people fleeing dangerous situations, hear firsthand accounts of violence or unrest, and often witness the raw, unfiltered fear of those experiencing the crisis in real-time. These posts can be shared and reshared, going viral and spreading panic quickly, sometimes without the necessary context or verification. Our feeds become flooded with emotional responses, making it difficult to separate fact from fear, and as a result, our perception of the situation becomes skewed.

Again, this isn't about casting blame on the media. It's simply the reality of how information is consumed today. The way news is delivered—constantly, urgently, and sometimes sensationally—triggers our most basic instincts to prepare for the worst. This means that feeling anxious or worried about the state of the world is not only normal but a direct result of how we're wired to respond to perceived threats. The challenge is recognizing when our natural instincts are being pushed into overdrive by the constant barrage of media and learning how to manage that response.

This doesn't mean tuning everything out. In fact, staying informed is crucial, especially when it comes to understanding potential threats to your safety. But it does mean being aware of how the flood of information affects you emotionally and psychologically. Understanding that your worry is partly a product of how we receive news today can help you put things into perspective and realize that while the risks are real, they aren't always as immediate or unavoidable as they might seem.

So, if you've been feeling a growing sense of dread, you're not alone. The world feels more volatile now than it has in a long time, and it's natural to worry about what comes next. But there's a difference between feeling anxious about the future and allowing fear to paralyze you. While the risks are real, they don't have to control your life. The key is understanding the situation and knowing how to respond rationally if things go wrong.

Practical Ways to Manage Uncertainty

So, what can you do? The good news is you don't need to overhaul your entire life to be ready for the unexpected. You can take manageable steps—right now, today—that will make a real difference if civil unrest occurs in your area.

This book is designed to guide you through those steps. We'll start with the basics, such as understanding how unrest unfolds, how to secure your home, and how to stay informed. From there, we'll dive into more specific scenarios, like what to do if you're caught in a protest, how to communicate with loved ones during an emergency, and when it might be time to leave your home for safer ground.

You won't need specialized training or expensive gear to follow the advice in these pages. What you will need is a willingness to think ahead, make a plan, and stay calm under pressure. By the time you finish this book, you'll have a clear sense of what to do in a crisis, how to keep yourself safe, and how to avoid common mistakes that can put people at risk when unrest breaks out.

The Purpose of This Book

This book is not about fear—it's about empowerment. My goal is to give you the tools and knowledge you need to protect yourself and your loved ones, even if you've never thought about preparedness before. You won't need to make drastic changes to your lifestyle or become a survival expert. You just need to be aware, stay calm, and follow a few simple principles that will help you navigate any situation with confidence.

We'll cover everything from securing your home and gathering essential supplies to staying safe during protests or riots. We'll talk about when to shelter in place and when it might be time to evacuate, and how to do so safely. Most importantly, we'll break it down into steps that are easy to understand and implement, so you don't feel overwhelmed.

You don't need to live in fear of the future. By the end of this book, you'll be better prepared to handle uncertainty, whatever form it takes. You'll know how to stay safe, how to protect those who depend on you, and how to face even the most difficult challenges with clarity and calm.

Let's get started.

1
Understanding the Threats

The first step toward preparation is understanding the types of civil unrest and how they unfold in different environments. Civil unrest isn't a monolithic event; it can range from peaceful protests to full-scale riots, and the triggers for these events are often complex and intertwined. By understanding the nature of these threats, you can anticipate when unrest might occur, recognize the signs that things are escalating, and take proactive steps to protect yourself and your loved ones.

Types of Civil Unrest

Protests

Definition: Protests are public gatherings of individuals or groups expressing dissent or advocating for change. They are often organized around specific issues like social justice, political reforms, economic policies, or environmental causes. In many cases, protests are a natural and healthy part of a democratic society. They provide a platform for people to voice their opinions and advocate for change.

Protests are not uncommon, especially in urban areas where political, social, or economic movements tend to gain momentum. In fact, most of the time, protests remain peaceful and are managed in coordination with local law enforcement to ensure the safety of both participants and the public. Events like the Women's March or environmental protests are examples of large-scale, peaceful demonstrations that disrupt city life without posing significant danger to bystanders.

However, while many protests begin with peaceful intentions, they can become volatile if emotions run high, opposing groups clash, or if external factors—such as a heavy-handed law enforcement response—escalate tensions. It's crucial to understand that protests themselves are not necessarily cause for alarm. A peaceful gathering can be managed safely, and most protests will conclude without any major incidents.

Impact: Even peaceful protests can disrupt daily life, particularly in urban areas. Streets may be blocked, businesses might close early as a precaution, and public transportation could be affected if large crowds gather near major hubs. It's important to be aware of protests happening in your area to avoid inadvertently getting caught in the middle of one, especially if your commute or errands take you near popular protest sites such as city squares, government buildings, or financial districts. Monitoring local news and social media can help you stay informed about where protests are occurring, and when they are likely to start or escalate.

That said, the presence of a protest doesn't automatically mean you're in danger. If you're aware of one taking place, you can adjust your plans to avoid the area and go about your day. The key is knowing when a protest is showing signs of escalating into something more dangerous, such as a riot or clash with law enforcement.

Counter-Protests and Increased Tension

While protests in and of themselves are not always dangerous, counter-protests can complicate the situation. A counter-protest occurs when an opposing group organizes a protest at the same time and place as another group to directly confront their message. These situations are inherently more volatile because they involve conflicting groups who may be highly emotional or even antagonistic toward each other.

When two opposing groups meet, the risk of conflict increases significantly. What might have been a peaceful protest can quickly devolve into heated arguments, shoving matches, or worse. Law enforcement presence usually increases during counter-protests to prevent violence, but this can sometimes lead to more tension as both sides feel threatened by the other or by police intervention.

Counter-protests are important to watch for because they are a strong indicator that a protest could escalate. If you are in or near an area where a protest and counter-protest are scheduled, it's wise to stay informed and be ready to change your route or even shelter in place if tensions rise.

When to Be Concerned: Recognizing Signs of Escalation

While protests are common and often peaceful, there are several signs that a protest might be escalating from peaceful demonstration to something more dangerous. Being able to recognize these signs can help you make better decisions about whether to avoid the area, leave early, or take other precautions to protect yourself.

1. Sudden Changes in the Crowd's Mood: If a protest that started calmly begins to see an

increase in shouting, aggressive body language, or confrontations with police, it may be a sign that tensions are rising. Watch for shifts in the crowd's energy, especially if the protest was peaceful for an extended period and then suddenly grows more intense.

2.   Increased Law Enforcement Presence: A notable increase in the number of police or military units in the area can indicate that authorities are expecting the situation to escalate. If officers begin to don riot gear or set up barricades, it's often a sign that they are preparing for potential clashes. This doesn't mean that violence will break out, but it does signal that the authorities are bracing for unrest. If you see these preparations being made, it's best to avoid the area entirely.

3.   Presence of Opposing Groups: As mentioned earlier, the arrival of counter-protesters increases the likelihood of a peaceful protest escalating. Opposing groups may begin with shouting or taunting each other, but this can easily escalate into physical confrontations. If you notice counter-protesters arriving, especially if tensions are already high, it's a good idea to move away from the scene.

4. Use of Tear Gas or Other Crowd-Control Measures: One of the clearest signs that a protest is escalating into a dangerous situation is the use of tear gas, rubber bullets, or water cannons by law enforcement. These tactics are typically used when authorities believe the crowd is becoming unmanageable or when they are trying to disperse a large group to prevent further escalation. If you hear reports of these methods being deployed, it's critical to leave the area as quickly and safely as possible,

as the situation may continue to deteriorate.

5. Vandalism or Property Destruction: When protests turn violent, one of the first signs is often the destruction of property. If you see windows being broken, cars being damaged, or buildings being vandalized, it's a signal that the protest is no longer under control. Rioters may target businesses or government buildings, but they can also damage personal property in the surrounding area. If you witness vandalism or looting, your safest option is to leave the area immediately, as these situations can escalate quickly into full-scale riots.

6. Aggressive or Panicked Behavior: The behavior of individuals within the protest can provide important clues about whether the situation is escalating. Watch for signs of panic, such as people running from the scene or pushing through crowds. Additionally, if you see individuals becoming increasingly aggressive— either toward each other, toward law enforcement, or toward property—it may indicate that the protest is shifting toward a more dangerous event.

7. Blocked Exits or Streets: When authorities or protesters start blocking streets or exits, it can signal that tensions are rising. This could be due to an effort by law enforcement to control the crowd, or it may be a tactic by protesters to take control of a specific area. In either case, blocked streets or exits make it harder to leave if the situation worsens. If you notice that you're in an area where roads or exits are being closed off, it's a good idea to move to a safer location before further escalation occurs.

Staying Safe During Protests

If you find yourself in an area where a protest or

counter-protest is occurring, it's important to stay informed and remain aware of your surroundings. Avoid getting too close to the protest unless you are participating and understand the risks involved. If you are a bystander or just passing through, the best way to stay safe is to distance yourself from the event and stay alert for signs of escalation.

- Monitor Social Media and Local News: Real-time updates can provide valuable information about where protests are happening and whether they are escalating. Apps like Twitter, local news outlets, or neighborhood alert services can keep you informed about any developments, allowing you to adjust your plans accordingly.

- Stay Calm and Move Deliberately: If you notice signs that a protest is escalating, it's important to stay calm. Panicking can make the situation more dangerous. Instead, move deliberately and with purpose toward a safe location—either away from the protest or to a secure indoor space.

- Avoid Confrontation: Even if you feel strongly about the issues being protested, engaging in confrontations—whether with protesters, counter-protesters, or law enforcement—can increase your risk. If you are not participating, your goal should be to avoid conflict altogether.

Protests are a common part of modern society, and most are peaceful expressions of people's rights to assemble and speak out. However, understanding when a protest is escalating—and what signs to look for—can help you navigate these situations with confidence. The key is staying informed, being aware of your surroundings, and taking action when necessary to protect yourself.

Riots

> Definition: Riots are characterized by violent and chaotic behavior, often involving property destruction, looting, and clashes with law enforcement. Unlike protests, which are generally organized with a clear message or goal, riots tend to emerge spontaneously. They can be triggered by a single incident—like a police confrontation or a provocative action—or by underlying tensions that reach a boiling point.

While some riots start from peaceful protests that escalate, others can break out without any formal organization, particularly in areas experiencing economic or racial tensions. Riots can also be opportunistic, with individuals or groups taking advantage of the chaos to commit acts of vandalism or theft.

Causes of Escalation: Riots can begin when large crowds gather, emotions run high, and a single spark sets off violent behavior. For example, a confrontation between protesters and police, a property being damaged, or rumors spreading through the crowd can lead to rapid escalation. Additionally, factors like insufficient law enforcement presence or a perceived heavy-handed response from authorities can amplify tensions and lead to riots.

Impact: Riots pose an immediate physical danger to anyone nearby, with the potential for injury, property damage, or getting caught in the crossfire between rioters and law enforcement. Riots can spread quickly across urban areas, affecting businesses, public transportation, and infrastructure. The longer a riot lasts, the more likely it is to attract opportunists looking to loot or cause further damage.

The best way to stay safe in a riot situation is to

avoid the area entirely. If you are caught in a riot, the most important thing is to move away from the chaos as quickly and safely as possible. Avoid large groups, and don't engage with anyone who is behaving aggressively. If you're in a vehicle, avoid driving through areas where riots are known to be occurring.

Historic Example: One of the most well-known riots in recent U.S. history is the Rodney King riots in Los Angeles in 1992. These riots were sparked by the acquittal of police officers who had been filmed beating Rodney King, a Black motorist. The verdict ignited long-simmering racial tensions in the city, and within hours, large-scale riots broke out, leading to widespread property destruction, looting, and dozens of deaths. The riots lasted six days, causing over $1 billion in damage and reshaping the city's policies toward law enforcement and community relations.

Political Violence

> Definition: Political violence refers to acts of aggression driven by political motives, which can include targeted attacks on political figures, government institutions, or groups with opposing ideologies. Unlike protests or riots, political violence is usually planned and intended to cause significant disruption or fear. This can range from bombings and assassinations to coordinated attacks on government buildings or political rallies.

Political violence may involve militant groups, insurgencies, or even domestic terrorism. While less common in stable democracies, political violence can occur when political tensions reach a breaking point or when extremist factions attempt to influence the political process through violence.

Impact: Political violence is often more dangerous and disruptive than riots or protests because it targets high-profile individuals or institutions. If you live in a city where political rallies, government offices, or embassies are located, you may be more vulnerable to these kinds of attacks. Political violence can lead to lockdowns, military presence, and severe disruption to daily life.

For example, the January 6th, 2021, attack on the U.S. Capitol was a stark reminder of how quickly political unrest can escalate into violence. What began as a protest over the results of the 2020 election turned into a violent assault on one of the most symbolic political institutions in the United States, leading to deaths, injuries, and widespread concern over political extremism.

Being aware of political events in your area and paying attention to any signs of increased tensions can help you anticipate and avoid potential incidents of political violence.

Looting

Definition: Looting refers to the illegal taking of goods, often during times of civil unrest or natural disasters. Looting typically occurs when law enforcement is either overwhelmed or deliberately avoiding conflict, allowing individuals to take advantage of the chaos to steal from stores, homes, or businesses. Looting can happen during both peaceful protests that turn violent and during riots or natural disasters when societal norms break down temporarily.

Looters may be motivated by desperation, anger, or opportunism, and their targets are often high-value businesses or vulnerable residential areas. In some cases, looting is tied to feelings of economic disenfranchisement or frustration with the government or law enforcement.

Impact: Looting can cause significant economic damage, particularly to small businesses and local economies. In cities or neighborhoods that experience looting, it can take months or even years for businesses to recover, leading to long-term economic instability.

Looting can also spill over into residential areas, especially if homes appear unoccupied or vulnerable. It's essential to secure your property during periods of civil unrest, especially if you live near commercial districts or in areas where law enforcement may be spread thin.

Potential Triggers of Civil Unrest

Civil unrest can be sparked by a variety of triggers, ranging from political events to economic instability. Understanding these triggers can help you anticipate when unrest may occur and take appropriate action to protect yourself and your family. While unrest can sometimes seem to come out of nowhere, there are often underlying tensions that eventually boil over. Let's explore some of the most common triggers of civil unrest and how they play out in real-world situations.

Elections: Elections are a frequent source of civil unrest, particularly in politically polarized environments or countries with fragile democratic institutions. Elections can spark unrest when the results are disputed, when allegations of fraud arise, or when the stakes of the election are perceived to be exceptionally high. Campaign rhetoric, political rallies, and post-election disputes can all lead to heightened emotions and, in some cases, protests or riots.

Impact: Elections are a uniquely sensitive time, especially in societies with deep political divides. During contested elections, demonstrations are often organized by supporters of both sides, sometimes resulting in clashes between groups. Additionally, the perceived legitimacy of election results can drive anger and frustration, especially if there is a belief that the electoral process has been tampered with. In the worst-case scenarios, electoral unrest can lead to violence or attempts to undermine democratic institutions.

Elections that are hotly contested—where both sides view the results as existential—are particularly likely to trigger unrest. The 2020 U.S. presidential election is a prime example. As results were delayed and mail-in ballots were counted, protests erupted in several cities, and conspiracy theories alleging widespread voter fraud fueled tension. This ultimately culminated in the January 6, 2021, storming of the U.S. Capitol by supporters of the losing candidate, an unprecedented act of political violence in modern American history.

However, election-related unrest isn't unique to the U.S. In countries like Kenya, Venezuela, and Belarus, disputed election results have led to widespread protests, government crackdowns, and, in some cases, prolonged periods of instability. Even in relatively stable democracies, contentious elections can trigger protests, particularly if the results are seen as illegitimate by large swaths of the population.

How to Prepare: During election seasons, especially in highly polarized political climates, it's wise to stay informed about planned protests or rallies in your area. Pay attention to news reports about potential disputes over election results and monitor social media for updates on gatherings or unrest. If you live near government buildings or polling stations, be prepared for increased police presence and potential road closures. Plan alternate routes to work or home, and if unrest appears likely, consider avoiding heavily trafficked areas where demonstrations might occur.

Economic Instability: Economic instability, such as rising unemployment, inflation, or austerity measures, is a powerful driver of civil unrest. When people struggle to meet their basic needs or feel that they are being economically marginalized, tensions can rise quickly. Economic downturns often lead to protests or strikes, particularly when government policies are perceived to favor the wealthy at the expense of the working class.

Impact: Economic protests can start peacefully but often grow in size and intensity as frustration builds. For example, the "Yellow Vest" protests in France began as demonstrations against rising fuel prices but quickly expanded into a broader movement against economic inequality and government policies perceived to harm the working class. The protests, which began in late 2018, resulted in widespread property damage, clashes with police, and prolonged disruptions in major cities.

Economic instability doesn't just affect developing nations. In 2008, during the global financial crisis, Greece saw widespread protests and riots over austerity measures imposed by the government in exchange for international bailout funds. Similarly, Venezuela has experienced ongoing unrest due to hyperinflation, food shortages, and the collapse of its economy, with protests often turning violent as citizens struggle to survive under dire economic conditions.

In addition to domestic economic problems, global economic shifts—such as trade wars, oil price fluctuations, or the fallout from international sanctions—can exacerbate instability within a country, particularly if it leads to job losses, higher prices for goods, or cuts to social services.

How to Prepare: Economic unrest can affect everyday life in many ways, from transportation strikes and business closures to price hikes and shortages of essential goods. It's important to have a plan in place to manage disruptions. Consider stockpiling non-perishable food, water, and essential medications to mitigate the impact of shortages. If you live in an area prone to economic protests, stay informed about planned demonstrations and avoid protest zones. Additionally, keep an eye on broader economic indicators—such as inflation rates, unemployment, and government debt levels—that may signal growing instability.

Racial and Social Tensions: Racial and social justice issues are potent triggers for civil unrest, particularly in countries where systemic inequality or discrimination has persisted for generations. Protests against police brutality, racial inequality, and other forms of social injustice often spark large-scale demonstrations. These movements can remain peaceful but may escalate into riots if tensions between protesters, law enforcement, or counter-protesters rise.

Impact: Racial and social justice protests have a long history of igniting unrest, particularly in the United States. The civil rights movement of the 1960s, for example, was marked by peaceful protests as well as violent clashes with police and opposing groups. More recently, the 2020 Black Lives Matter (BLM) protests following the killing of George Floyd by a police officer led to widespread demonstrations across the U.S. and globally, with some protests remaining peaceful while others escalated into riots and looting.

Social media has amplified the reach of these movements, making it easier for protests to spread rapidly across cities and even countries. What begins as a local protest against an injustice can quickly evolve into a nationwide movement, as was the case with the BLM protests. While the vast majority of these protests are peaceful, the highly emotional nature of the issues at stake—such as racial inequality, police violence, and discrimination—can lead to confrontations between protesters, law enforcement, and counter-protesters.

Protests around social justice issues can be unpredictable in terms of their size and intensity, and they may occur in unexpected places. While urban areas are often the focal point, smaller towns and suburban areas have also seen social justice protests in recent years, especially when local incidents trigger national outrage.

How to Prepare: If you live in an area where racial or social justice protests are common, it's important to stay aware of local events and monitor social media for updates on planned demonstrations. Avoid engaging in heated discussions about these topics in public settings, as emotions can run high, and confrontations are possible. If a protest turns violent or if looting begins, stay indoors and avoid the affected areas. In situations where social justice protests are planned near your workplace or home, consider working remotely or altering your daily routine to avoid potential clashes.

Government Policies: Significant changes in government policy, particularly those that directly affect people's livelihoods, can trigger unrest. Austerity measures, tax hikes, cuts to social services, and unpopular reforms—such as pension changes or healthcare restructuring—often lead to widespread protests, especially if the public perceives these changes as unfair or harmful.

Impact: Policy-driven protests can be long-lasting and

highly disruptive, especially if they involve key sectors of the economy, such as transportation or public services. For example, in Chile, a 2019 hike in subway fares triggered massive protests that quickly expanded to include broader issues like income inequality and the high cost of living. These protests led to widespread clashes with police, looting, and the imposition of a curfew in Santiago.

Similarly, in France, labor reforms and pension cuts have historically triggered massive protests and strikes, paralyzing cities like Paris and disrupting public services. These movements can gain momentum quickly, especially when organized by unions or political groups, and can cause significant disruption to daily life.

In countries with weaker institutions or authoritarian regimes, government policies that curtail freedoms or increase state control can lead to more severe forms of unrest, including violent uprisings or revolutions. For instance, in 2011, Egypt's Arab Spring uprising was fueled by long-standing grievances about government corruption, police brutality, and economic inequality, leading to widespread protests and the eventual ousting of the country's president.

How to Prepare: If you live in a country experiencing policy-related unrest, it's crucial to monitor the political landscape and stay informed about potential protests or strikes. Governments may impose curfews, cut internet access, or restrict movement in response to widespread protests, so have contingency plans for staying in communication with family members and accessing necessary resources. Stockpiling essential items can help you manage disruptions caused by strikes or protests and being aware of alternative routes for commuting can minimize your exposure to unrest.

By understanding these potential triggers of civil unrest, you can better anticipate when and where instability might occur. While you can't control the broader political, economic, or social forces that drive these events, you can take proactive steps to protect yourself and your loved ones when tensions start to rise.

How Civil Unrest Unfolds in Urban and Suburban Areas

Civil unrest impacts urban and suburban areas differently, though no area is completely immune. Understanding how unrest plays out in each environment can help you anticipate potential risks and plan accordingly.

Urban Areas: Cities are often the epicenters of civil unrest, especially downtown areas where government buildings, financial centers, and protest venues are located. The dense population and high concentration of businesses and institutions make urban areas particularly vulnerable to protests, riots, and looting. In cities, the spread of unrest can happen quickly, with streets blocked off, public transportation shut down, and the potential for widespread property damage. If you live or work in an urban area, it's critical to stay informed about events as they unfold and be ready to shelter in place or evacuate if necessary.

Suburban Areas: While suburban areas are less likely to experience large-scale protests or riots, they are not immune to the effects of civil unrest. Looting, for example, can spread from urban centers to nearby suburban shopping districts. Additionally, suburbs may experience disruptions to infrastructure, such as roadblocks, transportation delays, or supply chain interruptions, especially if they are near a major city. If you live in a suburban area, it's important to keep an eye on nearby urban centers and be prepared for unrest to spill over.

Common Signs That Unrest Is Escalating

Civil unrest rarely erupts without warning. Whether a protest begins peacefully, or tensions are already running high, there are often clear signs that the situation is escalating. Understanding these signals can help you make informed decisions about when to leave an area or take further precautions to protect yourself. Below, we'll dive deeper into the specific signs that unrest is escalating, from changes in crowd behavior to the role of social media and the spread of unrest to neighboring areas.

Increased Police or Military Presence: When law enforcement or military units start to appear in larger numbers, it's often a sign that authorities are preparing for potential unrest. Pay attention to these movements, particularly if they coincide with protests, political events, or other gatherings.

Public Announcements or Warnings: Local governments or law enforcement agencies may issue warnings or advisories if they anticipate unrest. These can include calls for curfews, instructions to avoid certain areas, or general alerts about potential disruptions.

Sudden Changes in Crowd Behavior: Protests, even those that start peacefully, can escalate rapidly when the mood of the crowd shifts. Group dynamics can be unpredictable, and what begins as a calm, orderly demonstration can turn volatile with little warning. One of the most important signs that unrest is escalating is a sudden change in the behavior or tone of the crowd.

Crowd Psychology and Mob Mentality: Large groups of people often behave in ways that individuals would not. This phenomenon is known as mob mentality or "herd behavior." In crowds, individual responsibility can feel diminished, and people may act more aggressively or emotionally than they would if alone. When emotions like anger, frustration, or fear spread through a crowd, it can create a tipping point where people begin to act impulsively or violently.

- Group Polarization: In protests, people with similar grievances come together, and this shared sense of injustice can intensify feelings within the group. A crowd that starts with moderate demands can become more extreme as members feed off each other's energy and frustration.

- Deindividuation: This is a psychological state in which individuals lose their sense of personal responsibility and identity within a group. In large crowds, people may feel anonymous and, as a result, act out in ways they wouldn't normally, such as engaging in property damage or physical violence.

Key Signs to Watch For

Shifts in Chanting or Slogans: Protests often feature chants and slogans to unify the group around a cause. Pay attention if the tone of these chants changes from peaceful demands to more aggressive or confrontational language. A shift from calls for justice to calls for violence or retaliation is a sign that the crowd's mood is darkening.

Crowd Surges: A sudden surge in movement—whether toward police lines, barricades, or buildings—can indicate that the crowd is about to take more drastic action. These surges are often chaotic and can result in trampling or clashes between demonstrators and law enforcement.

Physical Confrontations: Any physical clashes between protesters and law enforcement, counter-protesters, or even individuals within the crowd can escalate quickly. If you notice shoving, throwing objects, or physical altercations, it's a sign that the situation is becoming more volatile.

Historical Example:

One historic example of how a peaceful protest can escalate is the 1968 Democratic National Convention in Chicago. What began as a peaceful anti-war protest turned into a violent confrontation between protesters and police. As tensions mounted, crowd behavior shifted, leading to several days of rioting. The combination of heavy-handed police tactics and an increasingly agitated crowd led to widespread unrest in the city.

Tips for Staying Safe:

- If you notice sudden changes in crowd behavior, especially if people seem agitated or aggressive, try to move away from the densest parts of the crowd.

- Pay attention to how law enforcement is reacting. If police begin putting on riot gear or forming defensive lines, it's a sign that they anticipate violence.

- Avoid getting caught in a crowd surge by positioning yourself near exits or escape routes. If the crowd begins to move rapidly, try to step aside to avoid being caught in the rush.

Social Media Activity

Social media plays a pivotal role in both organizing protests and fueling unrest. Platforms like Twitter, Facebook, and WhatsApp allow protest organizers to mobilize quickly, spread information, and coordinate large gatherings. However, these platforms can also amplify tensions and spread misinformation, which can escalate a situation even further.

How Social Media Predicts and Fuels Unrest

Real-Time Organization: Protest organizers often use

social media to coordinate locations, times, and logistics. This allows protests to form quickly and sometimes without much notice. Social media platforms like Twitter and WhatsApp groups are often used to rally people within hours, making it difficult for authorities or the public to predict where unrest will occur.

Misinformation and Rumors: During times of unrest, false information can spread rapidly on social media. Posts or tweets that exaggerate the size of a protest, falsely claim police brutality, or misrepresent events can cause panic and fuel anger. In some cases, fake news or manipulated images can incite violence by making the situation appear more dangerous than it is.

Echo Chambers: Social media platforms can create echo chambers where people are exposed only to information that reinforces their beliefs. In the context of a protest, this can lead to heightened emotions and increased polarization, making it more likely that individuals will act out violently.

Key Signs to Watch For

Calls for Confrontation: If you see posts or tweets that encourage violence, confrontation with law enforcement, or vandalism, it's a sign that the protest may turn dangerous.

Increased Aggressive Rhetoric: A shift in social media language from peaceful protest to calls for aggressive action—whether it's targeting government buildings, law enforcement, or businesses—indicates escalating tensions.

False Reports: Be cautious of dramatic claims or videos that appear sensational. If something seems extreme or implausible, verify it through multiple trusted news sources before reacting.

Practical Advice for Using Social Media During Unrest

Follow Reliable Sources: Stick to following established, reputable news organizations and local government agencies for updates. While social media can provide real-time information, it's important to cross-reference facts with reliable sources.

Stay in the Loop Without Panicking: Use social media to stay informed about developments in your area, but avoid getting caught up in fearmongering or conspiracy theories. Turn off notifications from groups or individuals who are spreading panic-inducing rumors.

Verify Before Sharing: Before sharing any information, verify it with a trusted source. Spreading misinformation can contribute to panic and worsen an already tense situation.

Unrest in Nearby Areas

Civil unrest can spread like wildfire from one city to another, particularly when there is a shared cause or common grievance. This phenomenon is often referred to as the "contagion effect," where protests, riots, or demonstrations in one location inspire similar actions in nearby cities or towns.

How Unrest Spreads

Shared Grievances: When unrest breaks out in one city, it can trigger a wave of protests in other areas, particularly if there are underlying tensions that mirror those in the original location. For example, the Black Lives Matter protests in 2020 started in Minneapolis following the death of George Floyd but quickly spread to cities across the U.S. and even internationally, as people rallied around the same cause of racial justice and police accountability.

Solidarity Movements: In some cases, protests in one city inspire solidarity movements in other regions. These solidarity protests can be peaceful or escalate depending on the local context. For instance, during the Arab Spring in 2010-2011, protests in Tunisia sparked uprisings across North Africa and the Middle East, including Egypt, Libya, and Syria, as people in neighboring countries sought similar political reforms.

Media Coverage and Social Media Amplification: News reports and social media coverage of unrest can inspire people in other locations to act. As images and videos of protests spread, people in other areas may feel compelled to join the movement, especially if they see their own struggles reflected in those of the original protest.

Key Signs to Watch For

Unrest in Neighboring Cities: If protests or riots are occurring in nearby cities or towns, it's wise to monitor the situation closely, as unrest can spread rapidly. For example, protests in a major city may inspire smaller cities within the same region to organize their own demonstrations.

Similar Grievances in Your Area: If the cause of the unrest—whether it's economic inequality, racial justice, or government corruption—is relevant in your community, it increases the likelihood that unrest could spread to your area.

Reports of Mobilization: Pay attention to reports of local groups organizing protests in response to unrest elsewhere. Solidarity protests, while often peaceful, can escalate if tensions are high or if counter-protests form.

Historical Example:

The Arab Spring is a powerful example of how unrest

can spread across borders. What began as a protest against government corruption and police brutality in Tunisia in late 2010 quickly spread to Egypt, Libya, Syria, and other Middle Eastern and North African nations. The shared grievances of corruption, economic inequality, and authoritarian rule created a domino effect, with each country experiencing its own version of mass protests, uprisings, and, in some cases, civil war.

Tips for Staying Safe:

•   Monitor Regional News: If unrest is happening in nearby cities, stay informed about whether it's spreading. Local news outlets and social media can provide updates on planned protests or demonstrations in your area.

•   Prepare for Disruptions: Even if protests haven't reached your town or city, be prepared for potential disruptions. Solidarity protests can lead to road closures, increased police presence, or business closures, even in areas that haven't experienced unrest directly.

•   Stay Away from Hotspots: If unrest is spreading to your area, avoid known protest hotspots like government buildings, city squares, or downtown areas where crowds are likely to gather.

Understanding these signs of escalation can help you make informed decisions about how to respond during periods of unrest. Whether it's noticing changes in crowd behavior, staying informed through social media, or recognizing the potential for unrest to spread, being aware of these indicators will allow you to take proactive steps to ensure your safety.

Historic Examples of Civil Unrest and How They Played Out

The Rodney King Riots (1992, Los Angeles):

After the acquittal of police officers involved in the beating of Rodney King, Los Angeles experienced some of the most intense riots in U.S. history. The unrest led to widespread looting, property destruction, and clashes with law enforcement, resulting in 63 deaths and over 2,000 injuries. The riots lasted for six days, and parts of the city were effectively shut down.

The Arab Spring (2010-2012, Middle East & North Africa):

The Arab Spring was a series of anti-government protests, uprisings, and armed rebellions that spread across much of the Arab world. It started in Tunisia and quickly spread to Egypt, Libya, Syria, and other countries, leading to regime changes, civil wars, and widespread violence. The movement showed how quickly unrest can spread from one country to another, driven by shared grievances and facilitated by social media.

George Floyd Protests (2020, Global):

Sparked by the killing of George Floyd, protests against police brutality and racial injustice erupted across the United States and spread to countries around the world. While many protests remained peaceful, others devolved into riots, looting, and violent clashes with law enforcement. In cities like Minneapolis, the unrest led to the destruction of businesses and significant disruptions to daily life.

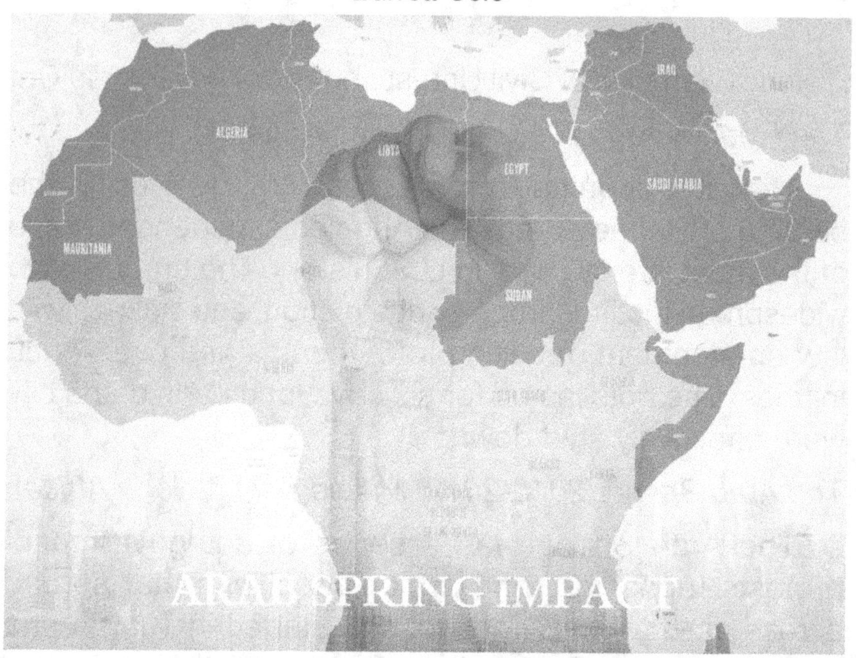

Understanding these types of civil unrest and their potential triggers can help you recognize when tensions are rising and take appropriate steps to protect yourself. While you can't predict exactly when or where unrest will occur, knowing the warning signs and being aware of how events have unfolded historically will give you a critical advantage in staying safe.

In the next chapter, we'll dive into the practical steps you can take to prepare for civil unrest before it happens, so you're ready to act when necessary.

2
Preparing Without Panic

Preparation for civil unrest doesn't mean becoming a "doomsday prepper" or living in constant fear. It's about taking reasonable, gradual steps toward being ready for unexpected situations. The goal of this chapter is to guide you through the basics of preparation in a way that feels manageable, helping you build confidence and peace of mind. By focusing on practical strategies, you'll be better equipped to handle civil unrest or other emergencies without panic.

How to Start Preparing Without Feeling Overwhelmed

Preparing for civil unrest doesn't have to be a daunting task that leaves you feeling overwhelmed or panicked. Instead, it's about taking small, manageable steps that gradually build toward a level of readiness that makes you feel more confident and secure. This section will help you break down the process of getting started in a way that fits into your daily life without causing unnecessary stress. By focusing on realistic, actionable steps, you can ease into preparedness at a comfortable pace.

Step 1: Start Small and Prioritize

When people first think about preparing for emergencies or civil unrest, it's easy to imagine worst-case scenarios and feel the need to rush into stockpiling everything at once. This reaction can lead to panic buying, overspending, and ending up with unnecessary items or supplies you might not need. Instead, start by addressing the most basic human needs—food, water, and shelter—and gradually build from there.

Prioritize Essentials First

Focus on the core necessities that will help you survive during a period of unrest when access to stores, utilities, or services may be disrupted. These essentials include:

- Water: Store enough water for at least one week (one gallon per person per day for drinking and sanitation). Start with a few bottles or a gallon and add more over time.

- Non-Perishable Food: Stock up on items that are easy to store and prepare, such as canned vegetables, soups, pasta, rice, and dried fruits. Aim for at least one week's worth of food for each person in your household.

- Basic Shelter Considerations: Even if you are planning to stay at home, ensure you have what you need in case of a power outage or damaged utilities, such as blankets, extra clothing layers, and basic tools for repairs.

Make a List of What You Already Have

You probably have some emergency items already—flashlights, a few canned goods, over-the-counter medicines, or a first aid kit. Take inventory of what's on hand before you begin buying anything. Knowing what you already have reduces the burden of starting from scratch and helps you avoid duplicate purchases.

Build Over Time

Preparation is not an all-or-nothing activity. It's okay to start with a small number of items and gradually build your supplies over time. For example, the next time you shop for groceries, pick up an extra pack of bottled water or a few cans of food. The following week, buy a small first aid kit or a flashlight. Spreading out the cost and effort will make preparing more affordable and less overwhelming.

Step 2: Set Manageable Goals

To avoid feeling like you need to prepare all at once, set small, achievable goals each week or month. This approach helps you make steady progress while still maintaining control over the process.

Example of Short-Term Goals:

Week 1: Purchase enough bottled water for three days per person.

Week 2: Add canned food and non-perishable snacks to your stockpile.

Week 3: Assemble or update a basic first aid kit with bandages, pain relievers, and antiseptic.

Week 4: Secure important documents (such as birth certificates and insurance policies) by making digital copies or putting them in a waterproof container.

These small goals make the overall process of preparing less intimidating and help build your confidence with each step.

Long-Term Goals

Once you have the basics, you can move on to long-term preparedness. This might involve having enough supplies for two weeks or more, purchasing additional tools like a portable stove or generator, or creating a more detailed emergency communication plan with your family. The key is to build upon each success, not to rush to the finish line.

Track Your Progress

Keeping track of what you've accomplished can help you stay motivated. You can do this with a simple checklist or by using an app designed for preparedness. Seeing the progress you're making will remind you that you're taking control of your safety and reducing the chance of being caught off guard.

Step 3: Integrate Preparation Into Daily Life

Another way to ease into preparedness is to integrate small steps into your everyday routines. This helps make the process feel less like an extraordinary task and more like a natural part of your lifestyle.

Incorporate Preparedness Into Grocery Shopping

When shopping for your regular groceries, pick up a few extra items each time that could be used in an emergency. Buying a few extra cans of beans or packs of batteries each week may seem insignificant, but over time, it will add up to a well-stocked supply without the panic or cost of bulk buying all at once.

Rotate Your Stock

Preparedness is not about stockpiling items indefinitely. Make sure you're rotating through your food supplies by using the oldest items first and replacing them regularly. This prevents waste and ensures you always have fresh, usable items on hand.

Check and Update Regularly

Just as you might routinely check your smoke alarm batteries, make it a habit to review your emergency supplies and plans on a regular basis. Set a reminder every three to six months to look over your emergency kit, rotate supplies, update important documents, and make adjustments as needed.

Include Your Family or Household

Preparation is a team effort. Involve your family members or roommates in the process by discussing your emergency plan, sharing responsibilities, and working together to gather supplies. This not only makes preparation more manageable but also gives everyone a sense of control and involvement.

Psychological Benefits of Preparation

One key reason to start small and prioritize is that the psychological benefits of being prepared will reduce your anxiety about civil unrest or other emergencies. When you know you're taking steps, no matter how small, toward readiness, it helps reduce feelings of helplessness or panic.

Shift from Anxiety to Empowerment

Preparedness is about empowerment. Instead of feeling overwhelmed by what could happen, you can gain confidence knowing that you have the tools and supplies to handle the situation. The more you prepare, the more secure you'll feel. This gradual sense of empowerment is especially important for those who are new to the idea of preparing for emergencies.

Avoiding "Panic Mode"

When civil unrest erupts or another emergency strikes, panic is the last thing you want. People who are unprepared often rush out to buy whatever they can, leading to empty shelves, crowded stores, and poorly thought-out purchases. By preparing gradually, you avoid these frantic last-minute efforts and can calmly focus on following your plan.

Creating a Practical Emergency Plan

An emergency plan is the backbone of any preparedness effort. It gives you and your household clear instructions on what to do if civil unrest escalates, ensuring that everyone knows how to stay safe and communicate during a crisis. This section will guide you through creating a realistic, actionable emergency plan that can be adapted to different situations without feeling overwhelming.

Step 1: Establish Communication Channels

In any crisis, clear communication is crucial. During periods of civil unrest, cell towers may become overwhelmed, internet access may be restricted, and misinformation can spread rapidly. Having reliable ways to communicate with family, friends, and emergency services will help you stay informed and coordinated.

Primary Communication Methods

Most people rely on their smartphones as the primary means of communication. While this is usually reliable, it's important to have backup options in case cellular networks go down or you lose access to Wi-Fi.

- Group Text Messaging: Set up a group text for your family or household members to use in emergencies. This allows everyone to quickly check in with each other. If phone service is unreliable, text messages are more likely to go through than voice calls.

- Messaging Apps: Apps like WhatsApp or Signal can be useful because they rely on data rather than cell service, making them more reliable if cell networks are congested. However, these apps require internet access, so they may not work if the internet goes down.

- Backup Devices: Consider investing in portable chargers (battery packs) so your phone remains functional during power outages. Additionally, walkie-talkies or two-way radios can serve as backup communication tools if cellular networks are completely unavailable.

Backup Communication Options

- Out-of-Area Contact: Designate a family member or friend who lives outside of your immediate area to act as a point of contact. In case local networks are down or overwhelmed, everyone in your family can call or text this person to let them know they're safe. This person can help relay information between family members who might not be able to communicate directly.

- Emergency Communication Cards: For children or elderly family members, create emergency contact cards with key phone numbers, addresses, and instructions. This is helpful if they are separated from you and need assistance from others, like neighbors or emergency personnel.

Check-in Times

Decide in advance on check-in times during unrest. For example, you might agree to check in with each other every two hours via text or phone to ensure everyone is safe. This minimizes confusion if the situation becomes chaotic.

Step 2: Identify Meeting Points

If civil unrest leads to an evacuation or a scenario where you cannot reach your home, it's essential to have designated meeting points where your family or household members can gather. Having pre-determined locations reduces the uncertainty of where to go if you're separated.

Primary Meeting Point (Near Your Home)

Choose a location within walking distance of your home where family members can gather if it's not safe to stay indoors or if there's a need to evacuate quickly. This could be a local park, a nearby school, or a community center. Make sure everyone knows the exact address and can navigate there on foot if necessary.

Key Considerations: The meeting point should be in a safe, accessible area. Avoid busy streets, protest hotspots, or locations near government buildings, as these could become targets during civil unrest.

Secondary Meeting Point (Outside Your Immediate Area)

If your neighborhood becomes unsafe or inaccessible, you'll need a backup meeting location farther away. This could be a relative's house, a friend's place, or another safe public area. Ensure that everyone knows how to reach this location by car, foot, or public transportation if needed.

Alternate Routes: Identify multiple ways to reach your secondary meeting point, in case roads are blocked or transportation is disrupted. Have printed maps or written instructions in case GPS is down.

Practice Your Meeting Plan

Once you've chosen your meeting points, practice how you'd reach them. If you have children, walk them through the route so they're familiar with it. Regular practice ensures that everyone knows what to do during an actual emergency.

Step 3: Plan Escape Routes

In some cases, staying put might not be an option. If civil unrest is escalating in your neighborhood, knowing how to leave quickly and safely is critical. Having escape routes planned ahead of time reduces the risk of getting caught in unsafe areas or roadblocks.

Local Escape Routes

Identify the fastest and safest routes to leave your neighborhood, both by car and on foot. You should have multiple routes planned in case one is blocked by protesters, law enforcement, or road closures.

- By Car: Know the main roads that lead out of your area, and plan for alternate side streets that might be less congested. Keep your car's gas tank at least half full during periods of potential unrest, and consider keeping an emergency car kit in your trunk (including a phone charger, first aid kit, snacks, and water).

- On Foot: In situations where driving isn't feasible, identify footpaths, parks, or pedestrian-friendly routes that lead away from crowded areas. Walking might be your best option if roads are blocked or if public transportation is suspended.

Regional or Long-Distance Evacuation

If unrest is widespread or particularly dangerous, you may need to leave your city or town altogether. Have a plan for reaching a safe location outside of the immediate area, such as a relative's home in another part of the state.

- Transportation Considerations: If you don't own a car, plan for how you would evacuate. Look into carpooling options with neighbors or relatives, or familiarize yourself with public transit routes that connect to surrounding areas. Have cash on hand in case you need to pay for alternative transportation.

- Lodging and Safety: Consider staying with friends or family in nearby towns if you need to evacuate. Alternatively, identify safe hotels or shelters where you can stay if needed. Research their locations ahead of time, so you're not scrambling to find a place to stay during an emergency.

Special Considerations for Vulnerable Individuals

If you have elderly family members, young children, or people with disabilities in your household, your emergency plan should take their specific needs into account.

- For Young Children: Teach children where the meeting points are and how to reach them. Create a simple version of the emergency plan that they can understand, including what to do if they're separated from an adult. Consider packing a "comfort kit" with snacks, water, a favorite toy, and a blanket to help children stay calm.

- For Elderly Family Members: Make sure elderly relatives have a way to contact you or others if they are alone. Keep a list of their medications and healthcare needs readily accessible in case you need to leave quickly.

- For People with Disabilities: Plan for transportation that accommodates mobility needs. Ensure any assistive devices, medications, or medical equipment are part of your evacuation plan.

Important Documents and Information

As part of your emergency plan, ensure that you have all necessary documents and contact information ready in case you need to evacuate or can't return home immediately.

- Digital and Physical Copies of Documents: Have both digital and physical copies of important documents such as ID cards, medical records, insurance policies, and property deeds. Store physical copies in a waterproof, fireproof container, and upload digital copies to a secure cloud service.

- Emergency Contacts: Keep a list of emergency contacts (family, friends, doctors, and emergency services) in both your phone and on paper. Make sure all household members have access to this information in case you're separated.

Practice and Review Your Plan Regularly

Creating an emergency plan is just the first step. It's important to practice your plan and review it regularly to ensure it stays up to date. Revisit your plan at least once every six months to account for any changes in your household, work situation, or local environment.

- Drills: Schedule practice drills with your household, including meeting at your designated points and practicing evacuation routes. This helps everyone feel more confident about what to do if an emergency arises.

- Update Your Plan: If your family dynamics change (e.g., new members or someone moves away), or if your neighborhood undergoes major changes (like new construction or traffic patterns), update your plan to reflect those changes.

Gathering Essential Supplies: What You Really Need

When it comes to preparing for civil unrest or any emergency, it's important to focus on gathering practical supplies that will help you meet basic needs, rather than stockpiling unnecessary items. This section will walk you through the essential supplies you should have on hand, including food, water, medications, hygiene products, and other key items to ensure your household can function smoothly during a disruption. The goal is to build a supply that's both useful and manageable, avoiding the stress of panic buying or over-preparing.

Food Supplies

Food is one of the most critical components of your emergency supplies. However, there's no need to buy huge quantities of food all at once. Start by building a small stockpile of non-perishable items that are easy to store and require little preparation. Aim for a minimum of one week's worth of food, gradually building up to two weeks or more.

- Non-Perishable Foods: Canned goods (vegetables, fruits, beans, soups, and fish), pasta, rice, lentils, oats, and dried fruits are excellent staples. Choose items that have a long shelf life, can be prepared without complex cooking, and provide essential nutrients.

  Examples: Canned beans, canned tuna, peanut butter, shelf-stable milk, boxed pasta, instant oatmeal, and snack bars. These items provide a mix of protein, carbohydrates, and fats, which are all important in keeping you energized during an emergency.

- Ready-to-Eat Foods: Stock up on items that require no cooking, such as granola bars, crackers, nuts, trail mix, and canned meals like chili or stew. This is particularly helpful if you're without electricity and can't use a stove.

- Shelf-Stable Comfort Foods: In times of stress, having a few comfort foods can provide emotional relief. Consider packing some items like chocolate, cookies, or instant coffee to help maintain morale.

- Cooking Without Power: If you have the space, invest in a small camping stove or portable butane burner that allows you to cook even if there's a power outage.

Be sure to store extra fuel and know how to use the stove safely.

Water Supplies

Access to clean water is essential, especially if civil unrest disrupts local utilities or water supplies. The general rule of thumb is to have at least one gallon of water per person, per day for drinking and sanitation. Aim for a supply that will last at least one week, and longer if possible.

- Bottled Water: Purchase bottled water or fill clean containers with tap water and store them in a cool, dark place. Water has a shelf life, so make sure to rotate your stock every six months to a year to ensure freshness.

- Water Containers: In addition to bottled water, consider investing in larger water containers (like five-gallon jugs) that can store more water and are easier to refill from a clean source if needed.

- Water Filtration: In case the water supply becomes contaminated, having a water filter or water purification tablets is an important backup. These tools can purify water from natural sources, like rivers or lakes, or even from tap water if it's compromised. Popular options include the LifeStraw or Sawyer Mini Filter.

Medications and Hygiene Products

Prescription Medications

If you or a family member rely on prescription medications, it's crucial to have an adequate supply during times of unrest. Pharmacies may close or become difficult to access, so try to have at least a two-week supply of essential medications on hand.

- Speak With Your Doctor: Ask your healthcare provider if they can prescribe an extra supply of medication to store in case of emergency. Some insurance companies may allow for early refills in situations where natural disasters or unrest are anticipated.

- Medication Storage: Keep your medications in a cool, dry place, and make sure they're clearly labeled. It's also helpful to keep a list of your prescriptions, including dosage and frequency, in your emergency kit.

Over-the-Counter Medications

In addition to prescription medications, stock up on basic over-the-counter medications that can help manage common ailments during an emergency. These include:

- Pain Relievers (ibuprofen, acetaminophen)
- Cold and Flu Medicine
- Antacids
- Allergy Medication
- Antidiarrheal Medicine

First Aid Kit

A well-stocked first aid kit is essential for handling minor injuries or illnesses when medical help may be delayed. Your kit should include:

- Adhesive bandages (variety of sizes)
- Sterile gauze pads
- Antiseptic wipes or solution
- Medical tape
- Tweezers and scissors
- Disposable gloves
- Pain relievers
- A thermometer
- Burn cream or aloe vera
- Antibiotic ointment

Hygiene Products

Maintaining hygiene is critical during periods of unrest,

especially if water supply or sanitation services are disrupted. Make sure you have enough personal hygiene products for each person in your household, such as:

- Soap and Hand Sanitizer: Keep antibacterial soap or hand sanitizer on hand to ensure you can maintain basic hygiene even if water is limited.

- Toothpaste and Toothbrushes: Stock extra toothpaste and toothbrushes for each family member.

- Toilet Paper and Wet Wipes: Toilet paper is a basic necessity, and wet wipes are useful for cleaning when showering is not possible.

- Feminine Hygiene Products: Ensure you have an ample supply of tampons, pads, or other products, depending on personal needs.

- Diapers and Baby Wipes: If you have young children, make sure you have enough diapers and wipes for several weeks.

Cleaning Supplies

In case sanitation services are interrupted, having basic cleaning supplies is important to maintain a clean and healthy environment. Consider the following:

- Bleach: A small amount of bleach can be used to purify water or disinfect surfaces (make sure you know the correct dilution for water purification—typically 8 drops of unscented bleach per gallon of water).

- Trash Bags: Stock heavy-duty trash bags for waste disposal, particularly if regular services are interrupted.

- Disposable Gloves and Masks: These can be helpful for cleaning up debris, handling waste, or protecting yourself in crowded or unsanitary environments.

Miscellaneous Essentials

Flashlights and Batteries

A reliable source of light is critical in case of power outages, especially during the night. Make sure you have:

- Flashlights: Invest in a few high-quality flashlights for each member of your household, as well as one for each main room in your home.

- Headlamps: Headlamps are a hands-free option that can be very useful during emergencies.

- Batteries: Stock up on extra batteries for your flashlights, radio, and any other devices that might require them.

Portable Radio

Having a battery-powered or hand-crank radio can help you stay informed when phone lines or the internet are down. Many emergency radios are equipped with features like NOAA weather updates and flashlight capabilities. This ensures that you can receive important news and emergency alerts, even if modern technology isn't working.

Cash

In times of unrest, ATMs may not be functional, and electronic payment systems can be unreliable. Keep a small amount of cash on hand, ideally in small denominations, so you can make purchases even if card systems are down. This is especially important for purchasing food, gas, or other essentials when credit and debit transactions aren't an option.

Clothing and Blankets

If unrest or power outages force you to leave your home or stay without heat, having extra layers of warm clothing and blankets is essential. Prepare the following:

- Weather-Appropriate Clothing: Stock extra socks, jackets, hats, and gloves if you live in colder climates. If it's summer, have lightweight, breathable clothing and sun protection.

- Blankets and Sleeping Bags: Store blankets or sleeping bags that provide warmth if you're without electricity during cold weather or if you're forced to sleep in your car or outside.

Building a Go-Bag

In addition to your general emergency supplies, consider assembling a "go-bag"—a small backpack or duffel bag packed with the essentials you'd need if you had to evacuate your home quickly. This is especially important in case civil unrest escalates to the point where staying home isn't safe.

Key Items for Your Go-Bag

- Important Documents: Copies of IDs, insurance information, and important contact numbers.

- Food and Water: Pack some high-energy, non-perishable food like protein bars, and include a water bottle or a small portable water filter.

- Clothing: Include a change of clothes, including socks and underwear, appropriate for the season.

- First Aid Kit: A small version of your larger first aid kit with basic supplies.

- Cash: Keep some cash in small bills.

- Flashlight and Batteries: A compact flashlight with extra batteries.

- Basic Hygiene Items: Toothbrush, toothpaste, hand sanitizer, and wet wipes.

- Portable Phone Charger: A fully charged power bank

for your phone or other small devices.

Digital Preparedness: *Backing Up Documents, Securing Your Online Identity, and Staying Informed*

In today's world, digital preparedness is just as crucial as having physical supplies. From backing up important documents to securing your online identity, the digital aspect of emergency planning ensures you're not only physically safe but also able to manage essential information during a crisis. This section will guide you through the steps to protect your digital presence, ensure you have access to important documents, and stay informed in a fast-moving situation.

Backing Up Important Documents

In the event of civil unrest or any emergency, having access to important personal and financial documents can make a significant difference in how quickly you recover. While physical copies are necessary, digital backups ensure that you can access these documents even if you need to leave your home or lose access to your files.

Step 1: Identify Key Documents to Back Up

Start by making a list of the most important documents you would need during an emergency. These may include:

- Identification: Passports, driver's licenses, Social Security cards, birth certificates.

- Financial Documents: Bank account information, credit card statements, mortgage or lease agreements.

- Insurance Policies: Health, home, auto, life insurance policies.

- Medical Records: Prescription information, vaccination records, health history, doctor's contact information.

- Legal Documents: Wills, power of attorney, custody

agreements, property deeds, and other legal contracts.

- Emergency Contacts: A list of important phone numbers, including family, friends, doctors, and emergency services.

Step 2: Create Digital Copies

Once you've identified the essential documents, make digital copies of each one. You can scan or take clear photographs of the documents using your smartphone or a scanner. Ensure the digital copies are of high enough quality that they are legible and can be printed if necessary.

Step 3: Store Digital Copies Securely

Storing your digital documents in a secure, accessible place is vital. You have several options depending on your preferences and level of technical comfort:

- Cloud Storage: Services like Google Drive, Dropbox, or iCloud allow you to store digital files securely online. The benefit of using cloud storage is that you can access your files from any device with an internet connection. Make sure to set up two-factor authentication (2FA) on your cloud accounts for added security.

- Encrypted USB Drives: If you prefer not to store sensitive information in the cloud, consider using an encrypted USB drive. You can load your documents onto the drive, and the encryption ensures that only someone with the correct password can access the files. Keep the drive in a secure place, like a fireproof, waterproof safe.

- External Hard Drives: Similar to USB drives, external hard drives provide more storage space and can be a backup for larger sets of data. Make sure the hard drive is kept in a safe, secure location and only connect it to trusted computers.

Step 4: Maintain and Update Your Backup Regularly

Review your digital backup periodically (every 6 months to a year) to ensure all documents are up to date. If you've moved, renewed your passport, or changed any legal documents, update the digital versions accordingly. It's also a good idea to double-check that your storage method (cloud or physical drive) is still secure and accessible.

Securing Your Online Identity

During periods of civil unrest, cybercrime tends to spike as malicious actors take advantage of the confusion. In addition to protecting your physical well-being, you need to secure your online presence and identity to prevent theft or fraud. A compromised digital identity during a crisis can make recovery even more challenging.

Step 1: Strengthen Passwords and Use a Password Manager

One of the simplest and most effective ways to secure your online accounts is to use strong, unique passwords for each account. A strong password should:

- Be at least 12-16 characters long.

- Include a mix of uppercase and lowercase letters, numbers, and symbols.

- Avoid using easily guessable information (e.g., birthdays, names of family members, or common phrases).

Since creating and remembering multiple strong passwords can be difficult, use a password manager like LastPass, Dashlane, or 1Password. These services generate and store complex passwords for you, so you don't have to remember each one. They also allow you to access your accounts securely from multiple devices.

Step 2: Enable Two-Factor Authentication (2FA)

Two-factor authentication adds an extra layer of security to your accounts by requiring not only a password but also a second form of identification (like a code sent to your phone). Even if someone steals your password, they won't be able to access your account without this second verification step.

Set up 2FA on your most important accounts, including:

- Email Accounts: Email is often the gateway to other accounts (like banking or social media), so securing it with 2FA is critical.

- Banking and Financial Accounts: Protect your financial information by enabling 2FA on your bank and credit card accounts.

- Social Media Accounts: Social media accounts are often targeted for hacking, especially during periods of unrest when misinformation and scams are rampant. Securing these accounts can prevent unauthorized access.

Step 3: Be Cautious of Phishing Scams

Phishing scams often increase during times of crisis, as cybercriminals attempt to exploit fear and confusion. These scams usually come in the form of emails or texts pretending to be from legitimate organizations (banks, charities, government agencies) and ask you to click a link or provide personal information.

- How to Spot Phishing: Be wary of unsolicited messages asking for sensitive information, such as your login credentials or Social Security number. Legitimate organizations won't ask for this information via email or text.

- Verify Before You Click: Always verify the sender's email address or phone number. Hover over links in emails to see where they lead before clicking on them. If something seems suspicious, don't click. Instead, contact the company or organization directly through their official website or phone number.

Step 4: Back Up Important Online Accounts

In addition to protecting your accounts with strong passwords and 2FA, regularly back up the data from your most important online accounts. This is especially important for:

- Email: Back up important emails, contacts, and files from your email accounts. Most email providers allow you to download an archive of your data.

- Banking Information: Print or download your recent bank statements and transaction history to ensure you have a record if you're temporarily locked out of your account.

- Social Media: If you rely on social media for professional or personal purposes, consider downloading an archive of your posts, contacts, and messages. This can be useful if your account is hacked or if the platform experiences outages.

Staying Informed During a Crisis

Staying informed is one of the most important aspects of emergency preparedness. During periods of unrest, information can change rapidly, and it's crucial to have access to reliable news and updates. Knowing what's happening around you helps you make informed decisions and avoid danger.

Step 1: Follow Trusted News Sources

In times of civil unrest, misinformation and rumors spread quickly, especially on social media. To avoid panic or acting on false information, follow reliable news outlets and government agencies for updates.

- Local News: Keep an eye on your local news channels and radio stations, as they will often provide the most relevant information about your area, such as curfews, road closures, and areas to avoid.

- National and International News: Major news outlets like the BBC, NPR, or Reuters provide broader coverage of unrest that could affect multiple areas. These outlets also tend to verify information before reporting it, reducing the likelihood of spreading rumors.

- Government Alerts: Many local governments have alert systems that notify you via text or email about emergencies, including civil unrest. Sign up for these alerts through your city or state's official website.

Step 2: Use Social Media Wisely

While social media can be useful for real-time updates, it's also prone to spreading misinformation. Here's how to use it effectively:

- Follow Official Accounts: Follow government agencies, emergency services, and reputable journalists on platforms like Twitter or Facebook to get timely and accurate updates.

- Verify Before Sharing: Before sharing any information, check its source. If it's not from a verified or official account, double-check with another trusted source before spreading it further.

- Use Hashtags with Caution: During unrest, hashtags can help you follow developments in your area. However, be cautious about relying solely on hashtagged posts, as they are often unverified.

Step 3: Invest in an Emergency Radio

If phone lines and the internet are down, a battery-powered or hand-crank radio can be a lifesaver. Emergency radios can tune in to NOAA weather alerts and emergency broadcasts, giving you up-to-date information when digital channels are unavailable.

Step 4: Know When to Disconnect

During periods of unrest, it's easy to become overwhelmed by constant updates and the barrage of news, social media posts, and alerts. While it's important to stay informed, it's equally important to recognize when you need to take a break from the constant stream of information.

- Set Check-In Times: Instead of constantly scrolling, set specific times during the day to check the news or your social media feeds. This helps prevent anxiety and allows you to focus on other important tasks, like making sure your supplies and plans are in order.

- Use Distraction Tools: Apps or browser extensions that limit your time on social media can help you avoid the endless cycle of news and alerts that can lead to panic or fatigue.

Review and Update Your Digital Preparedness Regularly

Just as you would with your physical emergency supplies, it's important to review your digital preparedness regularly. Set a reminder every six months to:

- Update passwords and security settings on your accounts.

- Back up any new important documents or files.

- Check that your emergency contacts are still accurate.

- Ensure your devices and apps are running the latest security updates.

Mental Preparation: *Maintaining Calm and Reducing*

Anxiety During Unrest

One of the most overlooked yet essential parts of preparing for civil unrest is mental preparation. Having the right supplies and a plan in place is important, but remaining calm and composed in a crisis is equally critical. By building mental resilience and reducing anxiety, you can make better decisions, keep yourself and your loved ones safe, and avoid the pitfalls of panic. This section provides strategies for maintaining calm, dealing with stress, and mentally preparing for the unexpected.

The Importance of Mental Preparation

Mental preparation isn't just about staying calm in the moment; it's about building long-term resilience to handle high-stress situations with clarity and confidence. Civil unrest can be unpredictable and fast-moving, which can easily lead to feelings of fear, anxiety, or helplessness. By mentally preparing, you're training your mind to stay focused, make rational decisions, and prevent panic from taking over.

Why Mental Preparation Matters

- Clearer Decision-Making: In high-stress situations, the brain's "fight or flight" response can lead to impulsive decisions that may not be in your best interest. When you're mentally prepared, you can slow down, assess the situation, and make more informed choices.

- Emotional Stability: Civil unrest can trigger strong emotional reactions—fear, anger, frustration—which can make it harder to stay calm. Mental preparation helps you regulate these emotions and stay grounded.

- Resilience in the Face of Uncertainty: Uncertainty fuels anxiety. By preparing mentally, you can train yourself to handle uncertainty with a sense of control, knowing that you have the tools and strategies to manage the situation.

Techniques for Reducing Anxiety

Anxiety during periods of unrest is natural, but it's important to manage it before it becomes overwhelming. These techniques can help reduce anxiety and prevent stress from interfering with your ability to respond effectively.

1. Mindfulness and Breathing Exercises

Mindfulness helps ground you in the present moment, reducing feelings of fear or panic about what might happen. A key part of mindfulness is focusing on your breath, which helps calm the body's stress response. Here's a simple breathing exercise you can practice:

Deep Breathing Technique: Sit comfortably in a quiet place and close your eyes. Inhale slowly through your nose for a count of four, hold your breath for a count of four, then exhale through your mouth for a count of four. Repeat this process for several minutes, focusing only on your breath. This can help lower your heart rate, reduce anxiety, and refocus your mind.

Practicing mindfulness and breathing exercises regularly—before a crisis happens—will make it easier to calm yourself in high-pressure situations.

2. Cognitive Reframing

When you're anxious, your mind can get caught in negative thought loops, imagining worst-case scenarios and fueling more anxiety. Cognitive reframing is a technique that helps you shift these negative thoughts into more balanced, realistic ones.

Reframing Example: Instead of thinking, "I'll never be able to handle civil unrest," reframe it as, "I have prepared for this, and I can take steps to stay safe." This simple shift in perspective reminds you of the control you do have in a situation, rather than fixating on what's out of your control.

3. Setting Boundaries for Media Consumption

One of the biggest contributors to anxiety during civil unrest is the constant flow of information—often overwhelming and sensationalized—through the news and social media. While staying informed is important, consuming too much can increase stress and fear. Here's how to manage your media consumption:

Limit Your News Intake: Set specific times during the day to check the news, rather than continuously scrolling or watching updates. For example, limit your news checks to twice a day—once in the morning and once in the evening.

Curate Your Sources: Stick to reliable, fact-based news outlets and avoid alarmist or sensational sources that may increase your anxiety.

Take Breaks from Social Media: Social media can be a major source of misinformation and heightened emotions. Consider taking regular breaks or using apps that limit your time on social platforms to prevent being overwhelmed by constant updates.

Building Mental Resilience Over Time

Mental resilience isn't built overnight, but by practicing certain strategies consistently, you can strengthen your ability to cope with stress and uncertainty. The more resilient you become, the better equipped you'll be to handle civil unrest and other emergencies.

1. Practice Problem-Solving Skills

In times of crisis, knowing how to quickly assess a situation and come up with a solution is critical. Problem-solving skills help you stay proactive rather than reactive. One way to build these skills is through "mental rehearsals."

Mental Rehearsal: Imagine a potential crisis scenario—such as unrest breaking out in your neighborhood—and walk yourself through the steps you would take to stay safe. Mentally rehearse your plan, including how you would communicate with loved ones, where you would go, and what supplies you would need. This exercise helps reduce uncertainty and builds confidence that you know how to act when the time comes.

2. Establish Routines for Stability

During times of unrest, your regular routine may be disrupted. Establishing a new routine, even in the midst of uncertainty, can help reduce stress by providing structure and a sense of normalcy.

Daily Routines: Simple routines, like waking up at the same time, eating meals regularly, and taking time to exercise, can help anchor you during chaotic times. These small actions remind you that life goes on, even during periods of unrest.

Preparedness Routine: Integrating small preparedness tasks into your routine—like checking your emergency kit or reviewing your plan—can also reduce anxiety, as it reinforces the idea that you're taking proactive steps toward safety.

Dealing with Fear in the Moment

Even with preparation, fear is a natural response to dangerous situations. Learning how to manage fear in the moment is key to maintaining composure and staying safe.

1. Stay Grounded with the 5-4-3-2-1 Technique

The 5-4-3-2-1 grounding technique is a simple and

effective way to calm yourself in the midst of fear or panic. It helps bring your focus away from what's causing anxiety and back to your immediate surroundings.

How It Works:

- Identify 5 things you can see around you.
- Identify 4 things you can physically feel (the texture of your clothes, the ground beneath your feet).
- Identify 3 things you can hear (traffic, birds, people talking).
- Identify 2 things you can smell.
- Identify 1 thing you can taste (if nothing is available, focus on the sensation in your mouth).

This technique helps reorient your mind and body, shifting your focus away from panic and toward the present moment.

2. Box Breathing with the 4-4-4 Method

Another powerful technique for managing fear and anxiety is box breathing—also known as the 4-4-4 method. This breathing exercise helps slow down your heart rate, reduce stress, and bring your focus back to your breath, allowing you to regain control of your emotions.

How It Works:

- Inhale through your nose for 4 seconds.
- Hold your breath for 4 seconds.
- Exhale slowly through your mouth for 4 seconds.
- Repeat this cycle for several minutes, focusing on the steady rhythm of your breathing.

The deliberate, rhythmic nature of box breathing activates your parasympathetic nervous system, which helps counter the body's natural "fight or flight" response.

Practicing this technique regularly—both in calm moments and during stressful situations—can significantly improve your ability to stay composed when fear arises.

3. Control What You Can

One of the major causes of fear during unrest is the sense of losing control over the situation. Focusing on the things you can control—no matter how small—helps reduce feelings of helplessness.

Action Steps: In moments of fear, take small, manageable actions to regain a sense of control. For example, move to a safer location, call or text a loved one, check your emergency supplies, or practice a calming exercise like box breathing. Each small action reinforces your ability to manage the situation and reduces panic.

Supporting Mental Health During Extended Periods of Unrest

Sometimes, civil unrest can last for weeks or months, creating prolonged uncertainty. During these times, it's especially important to support your mental health and avoid burnout.

1. Stay Connected with Others

Social support is a critical component of mental health. Even during periods of unrest, it's important to stay connected with friends, family, and neighbors.

Digital Check-Ins: Use video calls, phone calls, or messaging apps to check in with loved ones regularly. Simply talking to someone can help alleviate feelings of isolation or anxiety.

Community Support: If possible, maintain communication with trusted neighbors or community members. Working together during a crisis—whether it's sharing information, supplies, or emotional support—

helps foster a sense of solidarity and reduces feelings of helplessness.

2. Focus on What Brings You Comfort

During times of uncertainty, focusing on comforting activities can help alleviate stress. These might include hobbies like reading, cooking, listening to music, or watching a favorite movie. Maintaining these positive activities provides emotional relief and distracts from the ongoing crisis.

Relaxation Techniques: Practices like yoga, meditation, or even stretching can help reduce physical tension caused by stress. Set aside time each day for relaxation, even if it's only for a few minutes.

Maintaining a Balanced Perspective

It's easy to let fear or anxiety take over during periods of civil unrest, but maintaining a balanced perspective is essential for making smart decisions. While the risks are real, reminding yourself of the steps you've taken to prepare can help counteract feelings of doom.

1. Focus on Preparedness, Not Panic

When anxiety flares up, remind yourself that you've already taken proactive steps to ensure your safety. You have a plan, you've gathered supplies, and you've mentally prepared for what might happen. This reassurance can help shift your focus from worrying about the unknown to feeling confident in your readiness.

2. Accept Uncertainty

One of the hardest aspects of civil unrest is the uncertainty it brings. While you can't predict everything that will happen, you can accept that uncertainty is part of the process—and that you have the tools to respond, no matter what comes next.

Empowering Yourself Through Mental Preparation

Mental preparation is a critical part of your overall readiness for civil unrest. By practicing mindfulness, managing anxiety, and building mental resilience, you can approach any crisis with confidence and calm. These skills not only help you manage fear in the moment, but also give you the emotional stability needed to make informed, rational decisions. Ultimately, by preparing your mind as well as your body and home, you'll be better equipped to handle whatever challenges come your way.

In the next chapter, we'll dive into securing your home and creating a safe environment for your family during periods of heightened unrest.

3
Securing Your Home

In times of civil unrest, your home becomes your primary line of defense. Securing your home doesn't have to involve expensive measures or extreme tactics. It's about taking practical, affordable steps to protect your space, blending into your environment, and ensuring that you and your family are safe. In this chapter, we'll walk through key strategies to secure your home without adopting a "bunker mentality," focusing on simple improvements, securing entry points, and low-key defense options.

Blending Into the Environment: Avoid Standing Out

One of the best ways to protect your home is to make it an unlikely target. During periods of civil unrest, looters or vandals often choose homes or businesses that appear vulnerable or stand out. By blending into your surroundings, you can reduce the chance of your home being singled out.

Keep a Low Profile

- Avoid Flashy Signs of Wealth: Homes that show obvious signs of wealth (luxury cars, expensive landscaping, visible electronics, etc.) are more likely to attract unwanted attention. Avoid keeping high-value items in plain view from the street or outside your house.

- Limit Exterior Lighting: While security lights can be useful, overly bright or excessive lighting may draw attention. Opt for motion-activated lights rather than constant floodlights, which provide security without broadcasting your presence all night.

- No Visible Preparations: Don't display things like boarded-up windows or stockpiled supplies unless absolutely necessary. These can signal to others that you've made significant preparations, making your home a potential target for desperate individuals.

Landscaping as a Shield

Strategic landscaping can help deter unwanted visitors without making your home look like a fortress.

- Natural Barriers: Consider planting thorny bushes or dense shrubs near windows or entry points. These natural barriers make it more difficult for someone to approach your home unnoticed.

- Privacy Trees or Hedges: Taller trees or hedges can provide a natural screen from the street, preventing passersby from seeing into your home.

- Gravel or Noisy Pathways: Laying gravel around vulnerable entry points can create noise if someone approaches, giving you a subtle early warning system without investing in expensive alarms.

It's important to note, however, that you should keep larger bushes or trees that might offer intruders a place to hide farther away from your house. Bushes that are too close to the home can provide cover for someone trying to break in, allowing them to lurk unseen. Position these barriers thoughtfully so they deter, rather than aid, potential intruders.

Securing Entry Points: Doors, Windows, and Other Vulnerable Areas

The most common way for someone to enter your home is through the front or back door or a ground-level window. Securing these entry points is crucial for home safety.

Reinforce Doors

Your doors are the primary entry points to your home, so they need to be as strong as possible.

- Install Deadbolt Locks: A strong deadbolt is a critical first step in securing your doors. Make sure your deadbolt extends at least one inch into the doorframe for maximum strength. Also ensure the doorframe itself is in good condition without signs of rot or excessive wear. The strongest deadbolt in the world does little good if secured to a rotten frame.

- Door Reinforcement Plates: Reinforce the doorframe and strike plate (the metal piece where the lock bolt enters) with heavy-duty metal plates. This makes it much harder for someone to kick in the door.

- Use a Door Barricade: Consider a door barricade, such as a security bar or a wedge that can be braced against the door. These devices make it significantly more difficult to break through, even with force, and are often a budget friendly option while still being highly effective. They have the added benefit of often not requiring any additional installation, so even the clumsiest of do-it-yourselfers can manage.

- Upgrade Door Material: If you have hollow-core

doors (common for interior doors), consider replacing them with solid-core doors for better security. Steel or solid wood doors are much harder to breach.

Secure Windows

Windows are another vulnerable point of entry. Simple steps can greatly improve their security.

- Install Window Locks: Many standard windows come with basic locks that can be easily broken. Upgrade these to more secure window locks, especially for ground-floor windows. Don't forget the windows in the garage if you have any. Often these are overlooked because they are rarely used.

- Window Film: Adding a layer of security film to your windows can help prevent them from shattering if someone tries to break in. This film holds the glass together even if it's cracked, making it harder to enter through a broken window.

- Use Dowels or Rods: Place wooden dowels or metal rods in the tracks of sliding windows and doors. This simple trick prevents them from being opened, even if the locks are bypassed.

- Plant Natural Barriers: As mentioned earlier, planting thorny or dense bushes beneath ground-floor windows can serve as an effective deterrent.

Secure Garage Doors

Garage doors are often overlooked as entry points, but they can be a weak link in home security.

- Reinforce the Garage Door: If your garage door is flimsy, consider reinforcing it with a brace kit designed to withstand force. Garage doors can also be secured with a manual lock or a heavy-duty latch that is difficult to pry open.

- Disable Automatic Openers: In times of unrest, it may be wise to disable automatic garage door openers, as they can be hacked or manipulated remotely. Switch to a manual locking system if necessary.

- Lock Interior Garage Doors: If someone manages to break into your garage, make sure the door leading from the garage into your home is locked and reinforced like your front door.

Affordable Security Upgrades

Securing your home doesn't have to be expensive. Many effective security measures are low-cost or DIY projects that can make a significant difference in your home's safety.

Security Cameras and Doorbell Cameras

- Affordable Camera Options: Basic security cameras have become much more affordable. Systems like Ring or Wyze provide motion-activated cameras with cloud storage that can alert you if someone approaches your home.

- Fake Security Cameras: If your budget is tight, installing fake security cameras can act as a deterrent. These look like real cameras but don't record footage, making potential intruders think they're being watched.

Alarm Systems

- DIY Alarm Systems: Many modern alarm systems, like SimpliSafe or Ring Alarm, offer DIY setups with no long-term contracts. These systems include door and window sensors, motion detectors, and even cameras, all of which can be monitored remotely from your phone.

- Noise Deterrents: Even if you can't afford a full alarm system, noise deterrents like motion-sensor alarms or door alarms that emit a loud sound when triggered can scare off potential intruders.

Reinforcing the Perimeter

- Motion-Sensor Lights: As mentioned earlier, motion-sensor lights are an affordable way to deter intruders. These lights only activate when someone enters your yard or approaches your home, which can scare off anyone trying to break in under the cover of darkness.

- Fencing: If your home doesn't already have a fence, installing a basic one can add an extra layer of security. Opt for a fence that's difficult to climb or see through, such as a wooden privacy fence or metal fencing with pointed tops.

Home Defense Without a Military Mindset

You don't need to adopt an aggressive, militarized mindset to defend your home. There are practical ways to protect your home and family that focus on deterring intruders and staying safe without resorting to extreme measures.

Defense Tools That Don't Require Lethal Force

If you're uncomfortable with firearms or lethal weapons, there are non-lethal options that can still provide protection.

- Pepper Spray: Having pepper spray in an accessible location gives you a means to incapacitate an intruder without causing permanent harm. Ensure that each adult in the household knows how to use it properly.

- Stun Guns or Tasers: These can also incapacitate

an intruder, allowing you time to escape or call for help.

- Personal Alarms: These small, portable devices emit a loud siren when triggered, which can scare off an intruder or alert neighbors to your situation.

Firearm Considerations: Understanding the Responsibility

If you believe that owning a firearm is necessary for your home defense, it's crucial to understand and respect the responsibility that comes with it. Firearms are serious, potentially deadly tools, and using them for self-defense requires significant consideration and preparation.

1. Know and Obey Local Laws

Before purchasing or using a firearm, it's essential to familiarize yourself with the laws and regulations in your area regarding firearm ownership, storage, and usage. Laws vary widely by region, and ignorance of the law is not a defense if you accidentally break it. Some areas have specific restrictions on the types of firearms you can own, how they must be stored, and under what circumstances they can be used for self-defense.

- Key Considerations: Research your local laws regarding firearm registration, background checks, storage requirements (such as using gun safes or locks), and the legal criteria for using deadly force in self-defense. Some jurisdictions have "stand your ground" laws, while others require a duty to retreat before using force.

2. Firearm Safety Training

If you decide to own a firearm, taking a course on proper firearm safety is essential. Firearms require knowledge, respect, and practice to be used safely and effectively. Training will teach you not only how to handle the firearm but also how to store it safely and use it under stress.

- Training Courses: Many local shooting ranges, gun shops, or law enforcement agencies offer firearm safety courses. These courses often cover topics like safe handling, proper storage, situational awareness, and understanding when the use of force is justified.

- Handling Under Stress: In a high-stress situation, adrenaline can impair your ability to think clearly. Regular practice at a shooting range can help you build muscle memory so that, if you ever need to use your firearm in self-defense, you're more likely to use it correctly and less likely to cause unintentional harm.

3. Safe Storage

Storing your firearm safely is just as important as knowing how to use it. Ensure your firearm is stored securely in a locked safe or with a trigger lock, particularly if you have children or others in the home who should not have access. Unsecured firearms increase the risk of accidents and theft.

- Firearm Safes: Invest in a secure, quick-access gun safe that prevents unauthorized individuals from accessing the firearm but allows you to retrieve it quickly in an emergency.

4. Understand the Seriousness

Firearms are not just another tool; they are deadly weapons. Their use in self-defense should be a last resort, not a primary strategy. Always consider other options—such as retreating, calling the authorities, or using non-lethal methods—before resorting to a firearm.

- Mental Preparedness: Owning a firearm for self-defense requires serious consideration of the emotional and psychological weight of using deadly force. It's important to understand the legal and moral implications of firing a weapon, and to be prepared for the consequences of such an action, even in a justified situation.

Creating a Safe Room

Designating a room in your home as a "safe room" can provide a secure place for your family to retreat to in case of a break-in or severe unrest.

What to Include: Your safe room should have a solid, lockable door, a communication device (cell phone, landline, or radio), some basic supplies (food, water, first aid), and a means of defense (such as pepper spray). Be aware that most interior doors on modern homes are hollow-core doors, meaning they are lightweight and relatively easy to break through. If possible, replace the door to your safe room with a solid-core door or reinforce the existing door with a security brace or door barricade to make it more difficult for an intruder to force entry. Additionally, consider installing a heavy-duty deadbolt on the door for added security.

Your safe room should also have windows reinforced with security film or shatter-resistant glass if they are present. This helps ensure that the room remains secure and provides more time for help to arrive or for the situation to de-escalate.

Room Location: Ideally, your safe room should be in a part of the house where it's easy to retreat to quickly. If you live in a two-story house, consider an upstairs room, as it's harder for intruders to reach.

Locks and Reinforcement: Ensure the door to your safe room has a strong lock or door brace and reinforce any windows in the room with security film or bars if necessary.

Developing a Community Safety Network

One of the most effective ways to enhance your home security during civil unrest is by fostering a strong sense of community. A coordinated neighborhood can act as a first line of defense, providing early warnings, sharing resources, and offering support during a crisis. Working together with your neighbors can significantly reduce the risk of your home or property becoming a target, and can create a safer environment for everyone.

Build Relationships with Neighbors

Getting to know your neighbors is the first step in creating a supportive community safety network. A strong neighborhood is often less attractive to outsiders looking to exploit unrest because there's a visible level of watchfulness and cooperation among residents. You don't need to become best friends with everyone, but having a basic level of communication and trust is key.

- Start Conversations: Begin by casually talking with your neighbors, especially those who live closest to you. Introduce yourself, exchange contact information, and let them know that you're looking to develop a neighborhood watch or communication system in case of emergencies.

- Share Contact Information: Create a list of phone numbers or set up a group chat with trusted neighbors to quickly share updates if there's suspicious activity, unrest in the area, or an emergency situation that requires attention.

- Host a Neighborhood Meeting: If possible, gather your neighbors for a simple meeting to discuss how to help each other in times of need. This could be as formal as setting up a regular neighborhood watch or as informal as agreeing to keep an eye on each other's homes when unrest is expected. Make sure everyone knows what to do if they witness suspicious behavior and how to report it quickly to others.

Neighborhood Watch Programs

A neighborhood watch program can be as formal or informal as the group is comfortable with, but the key is to establish some system of mutual support.

- Informal Watch Groups: Even if your neighborhood doesn't organize a formal watch group, having a few trusted neighbors who can keep an eye on each other's homes can go a long way. Discuss a basic system for how to communicate about anything unusual, such as texting or calling if you notice unfamiliar people loitering or suspicious activity.

- Formal Watch Programs: If your community is interested, you can organize a more formal neighborhood watch program in partnership with local law enforcement. These programs typically involve regular meetings, patrolling in shifts, and sharing updates on neighborhood safety. Many areas have pre-existing resources from law enforcement to help set up these programs.

- Signs of a Watchful Community: Homes in neighborhoods with visible signs of coordination and watchfulness are less likely to be targeted. Consider putting up neighborhood watch signs or motion-activated lights on homes, as these visual indicators can deter opportunistic criminals or vandals.

Using Community Messaging Apps

Technology can play an important role in community safety. Messaging apps like Nextdoor, WhatsApp, or Signal can help neighbors stay informed and quickly communicate in case of emergencies or unrest. Setting up a group chat or neighborhood page ensures that everyone is looped in when something happens.

- Real-Time Updates: With messaging apps, you can send out real-time alerts about anything suspicious happening in the area, such as unfamiliar vehicles driving around, individuals lingering near homes, or any reports of nearby unrest. This quick communication can help residents take precautionary measures.

- Coordination During Emergencies: In a situation where emergency services are slow to respond or overwhelmed, neighbors can coordinate to share supplies, offer shelter, or even organize patrols to keep an eye on the neighborhood.

- Information Sharing: These apps are also useful for sharing non-emergency information, like updates on local news, curfew notices, or closures due to unrest.

Pooling Resources

During extended periods of unrest, pooling resources with your neighbors can provide significant advantages. By working together, you can ensure that everyone has access to essential supplies and that the community is better equipped to handle disruptions.

- Sharing Essentials: You might not be able to prepare for every situation on your own, but if you and your neighbors pool resources, you can cover more bases. For example, one household might have a generator, while another has extra medical supplies. By sharing these resources, everyone can benefit from a collective safety net.

- Emergency Plans: Discuss with your neighbors what you would do if unrest escalates. For example, agree on a meeting point if evacuation becomes necessary, or plan how to help vulnerable residents (such as the elderly or families with young children) who may need extra assistance during a crisis.

- Mutual Aid: Consider creating a mutual aid network within your neighborhood, where neighbors can offer each other help with things like child care, food distribution, or transportation during times of unrest. This not only strengthens the community but also provides peace of mind knowing that you have a support system in place.

Strengthening the Community's Presence

A strong, cohesive neighborhood is often less vulnerable to external threats. When neighbors are visibly present and engaged, it sends a message that the community is organized and vigilant.

Visible Activity: During times of unrest, make sure to maintain a visible presence in your community. Walk around the neighborhood in pairs or small groups, check in on neighbors, and look out for each other. A well-patrolled neighborhood is far less likely to experience break-ins or vandalism.

Volunteer Patrols: Some communities organize volunteer patrols during periods of unrest. This doesn't mean confronting intruders but simply being visible and reporting suspicious activity to law enforcement or the group.

The Power of Collective Security

Ultimately, there is strength in numbers. A well-coordinated and supportive neighborhood can deter crime and offer much-needed security during times of civil unrest.

By building relationships, sharing information, and pooling resources, you create a safer environment for everyone. Instead of facing uncertainty alone, a strong community gives you the confidence that you're not just relying on your individual preparations, but on the collective safety and vigilance of those around you.

Final Thoughts on Home Security

Securing your home during periods of civil unrest doesn't require extreme measures or paranoia. By taking practical steps to secure entry points, blending into your environment, and preparing affordable defense options, you can protect your family and property effectively. Remember, the goal is not to create a fortress but to make your home a less appealing target while ensuring you have the tools and knowledge to stay safe.

In the next chapter, we'll explore planning your personal safety and mobility during unrest, covering how to stay safe when moving through the city, avoiding dangerous areas, and what to do if you need to evacuate quickly.

4
Personal Safety in the Streets

In the unfortunate event that you find yourself caught in civil unrest, maintaining personal safety becomes your top priority. The streets can quickly become unpredictable and dangerous during protests, riots, or other forms of civil unrest. However, you don't need to adopt a combative mindset to stay safe. This chapter focuses on situational awareness, making smart decisions, and using practical, non-confrontational strategies to protect yourself.

Situational Awareness: *Always Stay Aware of Your Surroundings*

Situational awareness is the most important tool for staying safe in unpredictable environments. It involves staying alert, understanding your surroundings, and being aware of any potential risks. Developing this habit can significantly reduce your risk of getting caught in a dangerous situation.

1. Stay Off Your Phone

One of the most common mistakes people make is being distracted by their phones while walking in public. During times of unrest, avoid distractions as much as possible. Stay off your phone unless absolutely necessary and avoid wearing headphones or anything else that could limit your ability to hear and observe your surroundings. Try to know your routes to and from the most important locations without having to reference the map on your phone. This could be extremely important in a fluid and dangerous situation. Always be aware of the best route to get home and an alternate route in case the primary route is unavailable.

2. Identify Potential Threats Early

Pay attention to what's happening around you. If you notice groups of people gathering, road closures, or changes in crowd behavior (yelling, shoving, or police presence), these are signs that unrest may be developing. Avoid walking into crowds or areas where tension seems to be escalating.

- Watch for Red Flags: Unusual police activity, groups of people moving quickly, or large gatherings can indicate that something is about to happen. If you see these signs, it's time to move to a safer location.

3. Have an Exit Plan

Always be aware of where your exits are—whether it's a side street, a store you can duck into, or a safe public space. If unrest starts while you're out, you need to know the quickest way to remove yourself from the situation. When entering buildings, take note of where emergency exits are, and if you're outside, avoid getting trapped in dead-end streets or enclosed spaces.

Blending In: *Avoid Drawing Unnecessary Attention*

When unrest occurs, drawing attention to yourself is the last thing you want. Blending in with the crowd or your surroundings helps you avoid becoming a target. This involves everything from how you dress to how you behave.

1. Dress Appropriately

During civil unrest, flashy or distinctive clothing can make you stand out. Stick to neutral, unbranded clothing that doesn't attract attention. Avoid wearing anything that identifies you with a specific political or social group, as this could make you a target for opposition groups.

- What to Avoid: Bright colors, logos, political slogans, or any other markers that make you identifiable.

- Blend Into Your Environment: Wear clothing that matches the area or crowd you're in. If the atmosphere becomes tense, you'll want to blend in with the general population rather than stand out.

2. Don't Engage with Crowds or Demonstrators

If you encounter a protest or a group of demonstrators, resist the temptation to engage. Even if you support the cause, getting involved can put you in danger if tensions escalate. Walk away from the crowd and find a safer route. If you're approached, remain neutral, polite, and keep moving.

3. Stay Calm and Move with Purpose

Panic attracts attention. If you find yourself near a volatile situation, don't run or appear fearful unless absolutely necessary. Instead, move calmly and with purpose toward a safe location. Running or showing signs of panic can draw unnecessary attention and increase your risk.

What to Do If Unrest Happens Nearby: *Stay, Evacuate, or Take Shelter?*

If unrest erupts close to your location, knowing how to react quickly and decisively can be lifesaving. Whether to stay, evacuate, or take shelter depends on the situation and your proximity to danger.

1. When to Stay Indoors

If you're in a building when unrest begins, your best option might be to stay inside and shelter in place. Lock the doors and stay away from windows, particularly if the unrest is happening in your immediate area.

- Shelter in Place: If you're in a secure building, staying inside is often the safest option. Avoid looking out windows, as you don't want to become a target for anyone outside. Stay calm and wait until the situation outside has de-escalated before venturing out.

2. When to Evacuate

If the unrest is escalating and there's a clear path to safety, evacuating the area may be your best choice. Move quickly, but don't rush. Evacuate quietly and calmly to avoid drawing attention.

- Avoiding Main Streets: If you decide to leave the area, avoid main streets or areas where crowds are likely to gather. Use side streets or less populated routes to get away.

- Have a Meeting Point: If you're with family or friends, designate a meeting point in case you get separated. Knowing where to regroup provides clarity in a chaotic situation.

3. When to Take Shelter

In some cases, you may need to take temporary shelter if evacuation isn't possible. This could mean ducking into a nearby store, office building, or any safe public space.

- Finding Shelter in Public Spaces: Public buildings, such as libraries or malls, can offer temporary protection if unrest breaks out. Look for places with visible security or police presence for added protection.

- Stay Inside the Building: Once inside, stay away from windows and doors. In extreme cases, moving to a secure room or lower level (if available) can offer additional protection.

Strengthening Your Home Defense: *Doors, Windows, and Garages*

While we covered home security in Chapter 3, it's essential to review how to strengthen entry points during times of civil unrest, especially when you need to make quick decisions about staying indoors.

1. Reinforce Doors and Windows

If you have time before unrest reaches your area, reinforce your doors and windows. Simple measures, like using door braces or placing dowels in window tracks, can make it harder for anyone to break in.

- Lock All Doors and Windows: This should be your first step when unrest is close by. Make sure all entry points are securely locked and reinforced.

- Use Window Film: If your home is in an area prone to unrest, security film can prevent windows from shattering if they're struck, offering an additional layer of protection.

2. Secure the Garage

Garages are often a weak point in home security. Make sure your garage door is locked and, if necessary, disable any automatic openers that could be remotely manipulated. Lock the door leading from your garage into your home as well.

Using Deterrents: *Lighting, Cameras, and Alarms*

Deterrents can be highly effective in discouraging

criminals or vandals from targeting your property. They signal that your home is protected and not worth the risk.

1. Motion-Activated Lighting

Motion-activated lights are inexpensive and effective. Install these lights around entry points, backyards, and side areas to deter anyone from approaching your home. The sudden light can startle would-be intruders and draw attention to their presence.

2. Security Cameras

Even basic security cameras can make your home a less attractive target. Doorbell cameras or cameras with motion-detection features allow you to monitor what's happening around your home from your phone. If you spot unrest or unusual activity, you can take action early.

- Cloud-Based Cameras: Some systems, like Ring or Wyze, offer affordable options with cloud storage, ensuring you can access footage even if your camera is disabled.

3. Alarms

A simple alarm system can make a huge difference. Whether it's a full security system or basic door and window alarms that emit a loud sound when triggered, these devices can deter intruders and alert you to any attempted break-ins.

Non-Confrontational Defense Options

While you want to avoid drawing attention or getting involved in unrest, you should still be prepared for self-defense if necessary. Non-confrontational defense options can provide protection without escalating the situation.

1. Pepper Spray

Pepper spray is easy to use and effective at disabling

an attacker long enough for you to escape. Make sure it's easily accessible, and practice using it so that you're comfortable deploying it in a high-pressure situation.

2. Personal Alarms

A small personal alarm attached to your keys or bag can be a useful deterrent. When activated, it emits a loud siren that can startle an attacker and draw attention, giving you a chance to flee.

3. Know When to Retreat

The most important aspect of personal safety in the streets is knowing when to remove yourself from a situation. Escaping danger and avoiding confrontation should always be your primary focus. Engaging with aggressors, whether verbally or physically, increases your risk. Whenever possible, choose flight over fight.

4. Fight if You Must

If your life is in danger, you have expended all options of de-escalation, you are unable to flee and you cannot call for help, you may have no choice but to fight back. This book cannot teach you how to do that. The best advice is to fight likc your life depends on it. It is not a movie, nor a boxing match. There is no such thing as "fair" or "unfair." There is win or lose and losing cannot be an option. If you do not have any formal training in how to fight, some basic tips you should be aware of include:

- Elbows and knees are less likely to break than wrists and ankles. That means striking with your elbow or knee will likely do more damage to them and less damage to you than throwing a punch or a kick with poor form.

- Aim for vulnerable spots typically left unguarded. Punches to the face look good in movies but are rarely effective in real life. Strikes to the groin, instep, kidneys and throat will be much more effective.

- The second you can create enough separation to get away safely, do it. Do not wait around to finish the fight. Flee at the first opportunity. Continuing a fight unnecessarily increases the chance of injury or escalation.

These tips are meant to offer guidance in extreme situations. Formal self-defense training is recommended for anyone seriously concerned about personal safety.

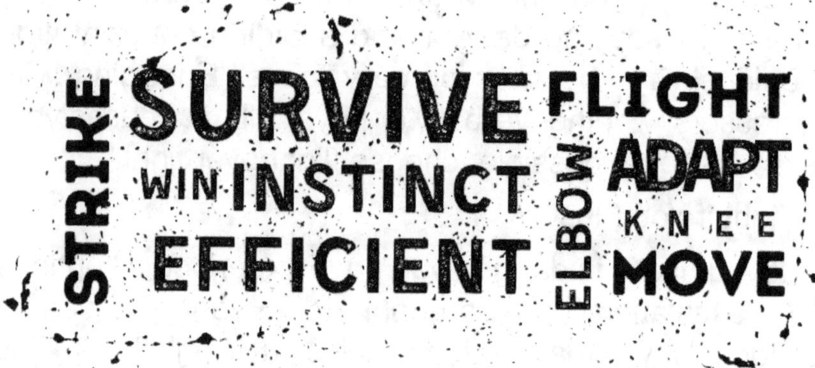

Final Thoughts on Personal Safety

Protecting yourself during civil unrest requires a combination of situational awareness, practical strategies, and calm decision-making. By blending in, avoiding unnecessary risks, and understanding when to shelter or evacuate, you can navigate even the most chaotic situations safely. Always remember: your safety is your priority, and avoiding confrontation is the best way to protect yourself and those around you.

In the next chapter, we'll explore how to stay safe during an evacuation, whether it's leaving your home due to unrest, natural disasters, or other emergencies.

5
Communications and Staying Informed

In times of civil unrest, reliable communication and access to accurate information can make the difference between staying safe and being caught off-guard. Whether traditional news sources are down or unreliable, or cell towers are overwhelmed, it's crucial to have a communication plan in place and know how to gather trustworthy information. This chapter will guide you through practical strategies to keep in touch with loved ones and stay informed, even in the most challenging circumstances.

Staying Informed When Traditional News Sources Are Unreliable or Down

During civil unrest, news coverage can be delayed, biased, or even completely unavailable. Mainstream media might not be able to provide accurate or timely information, or their servers could go down under high demand. Knowing how to find alternative sources of information is key to making informed decisions.

1. Real-Time Updates from Social Media

Social media platforms, such as X (formerly Twitter) and Facebook, are often the first to report on unfolding events. In times of unrest, users on the ground frequently post updates before the news outlets pick up the story. However, social media also carries the risk of misinformation, so it's important to cross-check multiple sources.

- How to Use Social Media Effectively: Follow local news stations, journalists, law enforcement agencies, and community organizations on platforms like X/Twitter or Facebook for real-time updates. Be cautious about unverified accounts or posts that seem sensational or lack credible sources.

- Hashtags and Geo-Tagged Posts: Searching for hashtags related to the event or location can provide additional context. For example, if there's unrest in your city, look for hashtags like #YourCityProtests or #YourCityUnrest to find localized updates.

2. Radio Broadcasts

When traditional outlets fail, radio is often one of the most reliable forms of communication. Battery-powered or hand-crank radios are indispensable during emergencies when electricity and internet connections are unreliable.

- Tune into Local AM/FM Stations: Local radio stations often have direct contact with authorities and can provide up-to-the-minute information about road closures, curfews, and safe zones.

- Emergency Radio Channels: Have a list of emergency radio frequencies (like NOAA weather channels or government emergency broadcasts) programmed into your radio for immediate access to critical updates.

3. Mobile News Apps and Alerts

Most major news outlets have mobile apps that send push notifications for breaking news. These apps can be a quick way to stay informed as long as your phone's battery lasts and the internet is accessible.

- Set Up Alerts: Enable notifications for breaking news in the app settings of trusted news sources. Choose local news apps for more specific, geographically relevant updates.

- Local Government Apps: Many cities and states have government apps that send emergency alerts or updates on local unrest, road closures, and evacuation instructions.

Alternative Communication Methods During Cell Tower Outages

Cell towers can easily become overwhelmed during large-scale emergencies or unrest, leading to dropped calls, delayed messages, or complete outages. Having alternative communication methods is essential to stay in touch with loved ones.

1. Text Messaging and SMS

Even when voice calls fail, text messaging often continues to work. SMS uses less bandwidth than phone calls, which means messages can sometimes get through even when the network is congested.

- Keep Texts Short: In a crisis, text networks may experience delays, so keep your messages brief and to the point. Avoid sending large attachments, which can further strain the system.

- Group Messaging Apps: Apps like WhatsApp, Signal, or Telegram use encrypted messaging and can work on weak data networks. These apps are useful for communicating with groups of family or friends when cellular networks are unreliable.

2. Two-Way Radios

For close-range communication (typically up to a few miles), two-way radios like walkie-talkies can be invaluable during cell outages. They allow real-time communication without relying on the cellular network.

- FRS/GMRS Radios: Family Radio Service (FRS) and General Mobile Radio Service (GMRS) radios are widely available and don't require a license for basic use. They offer a simple way to communicate with family members within a few miles.

- Battery or Solar-Powered Radios: Make sure your two-way radios are battery-operated or can be recharged with solar panels to ensure they work when the power is down.

3. Ham Radios

Ham radios, or amateur radios, are a more advanced option for communication in emergencies. While they require a license to operate, they offer long-range communication capabilities and are often used by emergency responders when other methods fail.

- Emergency Frequencies: Many ham radio operators provide emergency communication services during times of crisis. If you have a ham radio license, familiarize yourself with local emergency frequencies and keep your equipment charged and ready.

4. Satellite Phones

If you live in an area prone to unrest or natural disasters, investing in a satellite phone may be a good option. Satellite phones bypass traditional cell networks and connect directly to satellites, allowing communication even when cell towers are down.

- Reliable, but Expensive: Satellite phones provide

reliable communication during outages but can be expensive to purchase and maintain. They are typically recommended for those in high-risk areas or those who travel frequently to unstable regions.

Setting Up Family and Friend Communication Protocols in Emergencies

Establishing a clear communication plan with your loved ones can reduce panic and confusion during unrest. A well-thought-out protocol ensures that everyone knows what to do and how to stay in contact, even if traditional communication methods fail.

1. Designate a Family Communication Leader

Choose one person in your family or friend group to be the designated point of contact. This person will be responsible for relaying information and coordinating with others. Ideally, this should be someone who is less likely to be in a high-risk area.

- Role of the Leader: The communication leader should check in with all family members regularly, pass on important information, and serve as a central hub for updates.

2. Establish Check-In Times

Set specific times during the day when all family members are expected to check in, either by text, phone, or other agreed-upon methods. This ensures that everyone stays connected and knows when to expect updates.

- Example Protocol: Agree on a schedule where family members send updates at 9 AM, 12 PM, and 6 PM. If a check-in is missed, the designated leader can follow up.

3. Agree on Backup Communication Methods

If cell service is down, establish backup communication

methods. This could include meeting in person at a designated safe location, using two-way radios, or sending messages through a neighbor.

- Safe Meeting Points: Designate multiple meeting points, such as a nearby park, a friend's house, or a community center, in case communication fails entirely and evacuation becomes necessary.

4. Create a Code Word for Safety

Agree on a simple code word or phrase that family members can use to indicate if they are in trouble or need help. This code can be included in a seemingly innocuous message to avoid alerting potential threats.

- How It Works: For example, a family member might text, "I'm heading to the store for oranges" when they are in danger, signaling to the group that they need help or are in a dangerous situation.

The Importance of Local Intelligence: *Neighborhood Apps, Police Scanners, and Community Alerts*

While national news can give you an overview of what's happening, local intelligence is often the most important source of information during unrest. Understanding what's happening in your immediate neighborhood allows you to make safer, quicker decisions.

1. Neighborhood Apps

Apps like Nextdoor, Citizen, and Ring Neighbors provide local updates from residents in your area. These platforms allow users to share real-time information about incidents like protests, looting, or suspicious activity.

- How to Use These Apps: Monitor posts for updates about unrest in your area, including road closures, police activity, and safety tips from neighbors. These apps can provide hyper-local information that larger news outlets might miss.

2. Police Scanners

Listening to police scanners can provide real-time insights into law enforcement's response to unrest and potential threats in your neighborhood. While not all police communications are available to the public, many areas still broadcast general updates over public frequencies.

- Scanner Apps: Apps like Broadcastify allow you to listen to police scanners on your phone. These apps can be valuable during large-scale events, as they let you hear about roadblocks, curfews, and disturbances directly from law enforcement.

3. Community Alerts and Local Government

Many cities and counties have community alert systems that provide emergency updates. These alerts often include information about shelter-in-place orders, evacuation routes, and updates on local unrest.

- Sign Up for Alerts: Check with your local government's website to sign up for text or email alerts. Additionally, some areas use sirens or loudspeaker systems to notify residents of immediate danger.

Misinformation: *Understanding the Risks and How to Avoid It*

In times of unrest, misinformation can spread rapidly, fueling panic and poor decision-making. It's crucial to understand how misinformation works, where it's most common, the risks it poses, and how you can identify and avoid it. Being able to critically assess the information you consume can help you stay calm and make better choices during crises.

1. What Is Misinformation?

Misinformation refers to false or inaccurate information that is spread, often unintentionally. It can be the result of misunderstanding, misreporting, or simply mistakes made during fast-moving events. Misinformation is different from disinformation, which is false information deliberately spread to deceive or manipulate people.

During times of unrest, people tend to be more anxious and more eager for real-time updates, which makes them more vulnerable to misinformation. Even well-meaning individuals may share false information without verifying its accuracy, contributing to confusion.

2. Where Is Misinformation Most Common?

Misinformation is most commonly spread through social media, but it can also occur on news websites, messaging apps, and even word of mouth. The speed at which social media platforms allow information to circulate makes them particularly susceptible to misinformation.

- Social Media Platforms: Twitter, Facebook, Instagram, and TikTok are popular platforms where misinformation can spread quickly through posts, videos, and shares.

- Messaging Apps: Encrypted messaging apps like WhatsApp and Telegram are frequently used to share information privately within groups, which can include misinformation that spreads quickly among friends or family.

- Unverified News Websites: In an attempt to be the first to break a story, some websites may publish unverified or speculative information. These stories can quickly go viral, even if they are later corrected.

- Forums and Online Communities: Platforms like Reddit, 4chan, or smaller forums may also become hotspots for spreading misinformation, especially when users share content that isn't fact-checked.

3. The Risks of Misinformation During Unrest

The spread of misinformation during civil unrest poses significant risks. Inaccurate information can lead to poor decision-making, create unnecessary panic, and escalate tensions. Some of the risks include:

- False Alarm or Panic: Misinformation can cause people to panic unnecessarily, leading to chaotic decisions, such as rushing to evacuate when it's not needed, or staying in an unsafe location based on bad information.

- Escalation of Violence: In some cases, misinformation can spark or escalate violence. For example, a false report of police brutality, looting, or targeted attacks might incite a crowd or encourage more aggressive behavior.

- Diverting Resources: Authorities may have to divert valuable resources to address rumors or false alarms, making it harder for them to respond to real emergencies.

- Personal Safety Risks: Acting on misinformation can put you in harm's way. If you are misled into thinking a certain area is safe when it's not, or if false instructions circulate about how to stay safe, you could end up in greater danger.

4. How to Spot Misinformation

Identifying misinformation requires critical thinking and the ability to verify the sources of the information. Here are some tips to help you spot misinformation:

- Check the Source: Always verify where the information is coming from. Is it from a reputable news outlet or an official government source? Be skeptical of information that doesn't cite a reliable source or comes from an unknown or unverified account.

- Look for Multiple Reports: If a piece of information is true, it's likely that multiple reputable sources will report it. Cross-check information across different news outlets, both local and national. If you can't find the same information reported elsewhere, it's a red flag.

- Beware of Sensational Language: Misinformation often uses emotionally charged or sensational language to capture attention. If a post or article seems overly dramatic or is pushing extreme narratives, it may be designed to manipulate your emotions rather than inform you accurately.

- Check the Date: Sometimes, old news or past incidents are circulated as if they're happening in the present. Always check the date of articles, videos, or social media posts to ensure they're current and relevant to the situation.

- Reverse Image Search: Misinformation often uses misleading or out-of-context images. If you see an image that seems suspicious, use a reverse image search (Google Images or TinEye) to see if it's been used before in different contexts.

- Look Out for Confirmation Bias: People tend to believe and share information that aligns with their existing beliefs or fears. If a piece of information fits perfectly with your assumptions, take a step back and critically assess it before sharing. Just because it aligns with what you think doesn't mean it's true.

5. How to Avoid Misinformation

Avoiding misinformation takes a proactive approach to consuming and sharing information. Here are some best practices:

- Follow Trusted Sources: Stick to following official news outlets, government agencies, and reputable journalists for updates. Verified sources are far more likely to provide accurate information than random social media accounts or message board posts.

- Be Cautious About Sharing: Before sharing any news or updates with others, double-check its accuracy. Sharing misinformation, even unintentionally, only spreads confusion and panic. If you can't verify a story, it's better not to share it.

- Join Local Alert Systems: Many local governments or police departments have their own text or email alert systems for emergencies. These can provide reliable, real-time information during unrest or crises and are less likely to be influenced by misinformation.

- Use Fact-Checking Tools: Websites like Snopes, FactCheck.org, and PolitiFact specialize in debunking misinformation and disinformation. If something seems too outrageous to be true, fact-check it before believing or sharing it.

- Don't Rush to Judgment: In high-stress situations, it's easy to jump to conclusions or make snap decisions based on incomplete information. Take a moment to verify what you're seeing and hearing before reacting.

Misinformation is particularly dangerous during times of unrest because it plays on our fears and uncertainties. By taking a critical, measured approach to the information you consume, and verifying sources before acting on or sharing that information, you can avoid the risks associated with misinformation. Staying informed means staying vigilant about what's real and what's not and knowing how to differentiate between credible updates and unreliable rumors.

Final Thoughts on Communication and Staying Informed

In times of unrest, communication and accurate information are your lifelines. By setting up clear communication protocols, learning to use alternative methods when traditional networks fail, and staying informed through local intelligence, you can ensure your safety and that of your loved ones. Remember, the key to effective communication during a crisis is preparation— knowing who to contact, how to stay informed, and what to do if traditional methods aren't available.

In the next chapter, we'll explore how to stay safe during an evacuation, whether it's leaving your home due to unrest, natural disasters, or other emergencies.

6
What If You Need to Leave

In some situations, staying put isn't the safest option. Whether civil unrest is growing dangerously close, or the authorities have ordered an evacuation, you might need to leave your home or area. Evacuation doesn't have to be a panic-inducing experience if you've planned ahead and know how to travel safely. This chapter will guide you through the decision-making process, how to prepare for a potential evacuation, and what steps to take to ensure you and your loved ones remain safe on the road.

Recognizing When It's Time to Leave

One of the most critical decisions during civil unrest is determining whether to stay or leave. While sheltering in place is often the safest option, there are certain signs that it may be time to evacuate. Knowing when to leave can mean the difference between escaping danger and getting trapped in a hazardous situation.

1. Official Evacuation Orders

The clearest indicator that you need to evacuate is an official order from local authorities. If law enforcement or emergency services announce an evacuation due to escalating unrest, it's important to comply immediately.

They issue these orders to keep people safe and to reduce congestion and confusion in the area.

- Follow Orders Promptly: Don't wait until the last minute to leave if an evacuation is ordered. Crowds, blocked roads, and growing unrest could make it harder to get out later.

2. Increasing Violence or Danger

If unrest in your area begins to escalate—whether it's through violent protests, rioting, looting, or clashes with law enforcement—you need to assess your proximity to the danger. If your home or neighborhood is within striking distance of these events, it may be time to go.

- Look for Signs of Escalation: Is the unrest moving closer to your home or building? Are streets being blocked or is there increased police or military presence? If you see any of these signs, prepare to leave.

- Check Real-Time Updates: Use local news apps, social media, or police scanners to monitor the situation. If you're hearing reports of fires, looting, or road closures near your area, it's a good indicator that you should evacuate before it gets worse.

3. Utility Disruptions

Sometimes civil unrest leads to disruptions in essential services like water, electricity, and communication networks. If utilities in your area have been cut off for an extended period, and there's no clear sign of restoration, it may be safer to evacuate.

- Assess Your Resources: If you're running low on food, water, or other critical supplies due to utility disruptions, evacuating to a safer location could be the best choice.

4. Threats to Your Personal Safety

If there's a direct threat to your safety—such as looters in your neighborhood or personal attacks on your property—it's time to leave immediately. Don't wait for the situation to get worse.

Planning a Safe Evacuation: *Routes, Destinations, and Timing*

Evacuating during civil unrest requires careful planning. You'll need to decide where to go, how to get there, and the best time to leave. Proper planning reduces the risks associated with traveling during a crisis and helps you avoid chaotic or dangerous situations.

When civil unrest escalates to the point where evacuation becomes necessary, your ability to leave quickly, safely, and efficiently is paramount. While the situation may feel chaotic, thoughtful planning allows you to maintain control and avoid danger. Having multiple routes, a clear destination, and an understanding of when to leave can make all the difference.

Choosing Your Destination Wisely

One of the most critical decisions you'll make is choosing where to go. Evacuation doesn't mean fleeing aimlessly—having a pre-determined destination helps reduce panic and gives you a clear objective. Ideally, your destination will be somewhere safe, away from unrest, and capable of providing for your basic needs.

- Have Multiple Options: Relying on a single evacuation destination is risky. Unrest can spread unpredictably, making it crucial to have backup locations in different directions. For example, you might plan to stay with a family member in one town but also have a hotel or friend's house in the opposite direction as a secondary option.

- Choose Destinations Based on Risk: It's important to avoid heading toward known unrest hotspots. During political protests or riots, areas like government buildings, police stations, and downtown financial districts are often flashpoints for violence. Instead, seek out quieter, residential areas far from these hubs. If possible, consider destinations in smaller towns or rural areas where unrest is less likely to spread.

- Shelter Outside Your City or Town: In some cases, the safest place to evacuate may be entirely outside your city. If you can stay with relatives or book a hotel room a few hours away, it may offer greater security than trying to ride out unrest in your current location. If civil unrest appears long-lasting, consider longer-term arrangements in more stable areas.

- Identify Emergency Shelters: If staying with family or friends isn't an option, familiarize yourself with local emergency shelters. Cities often set up temporary shelters during crises, but it's important to confirm that these locations are safe and reliable. Local government websites or community emergency apps can help you find designated shelters.

Identifying Multiple Evacuation Routes

Evacuating during civil unrest is unpredictable, so you should always have at least two or three alternative routes to reach your destination. Crowds, police blockades, and accidents can make your planned route inaccessible at a moment's notice. Here's how to make sure you're not caught off-guard:

- Main Routes vs. Backroads: While major roads and highways may seem like the fastest option, they can quickly become congested during an evacuation. Protesters or law enforcement may also block these routes. Identify alternative backroads or smaller streets that could allow you to bypass crowded areas. Having several options in mind ensures you aren't trapped if your main route becomes blocked.

- Map Your Routes in Advance: Relying solely on a GPS system can be risky if the internet goes down or if signals are disrupted. Take the time to familiarize yourself with your evacuation routes ahead of time by driving or walking them to understand where obstacles could arise. It's also helpful to keep a printed map in your go-bag, as well as a downloaded offline map on your phone using apps like Google Maps or Maps.me.

- Use Real-Time Traffic and Safety Apps: Apps like Waze or Google Maps provide real-time traffic updates that can help you avoid congested or blocked roads. Citizen, Nextdoor, or local government apps may also provide updates on areas of unrest, so you can steer clear of protests or road closures. Be sure to check these apps before setting out and along the way to keep informed of any sudden changes.

- Avoid High-Risk Areas: If your evacuation route takes you near high-risk zones like city centers, police stations, or areas with ongoing protests, try to reroute before you get too close. Driving into a protest zone could trap you or put you in danger if the situation escalates.

Timing Is Critical

One of the most important factors in a successful evacuation is knowing when to leave. Leaving too early may feel premature, but waiting too long can expose you to greater risks. Knowing how to assess timing ensures you have a better chance of getting out safely.

- Leave Before the Situation Escalates: If you recognize the early signs of unrest escalating—such as road closures, military or police deployment, or reports of nearby violence—consider leaving before the situation becomes more chaotic. Evacuating early reduces the chance of getting stuck in traffic, encountering roadblocks, or facing direct threats.

- Monitor Local Alerts: Use your smartphone to monitor local government or news alerts about curfews, evacuations, or public safety warnings. If an official evacuation order is issued, don't wait until the last minute. Follow the instructions as quickly as possible to avoid becoming trapped by crowds or road closures.

- Avoid Peak Hours: If unrest occurs near your home or city, try to avoid evacuating during peak hours when roads are more likely to be congested. Instead, aim to travel during early morning or late evening hours, when fewer people are on the road, and the streets may be quieter. If you're monitoring protests, consider evacuating when demonstrations are likely to be paused or less active.

Recognizing when it's time to go is a critical part of ensuring your own safety and that of those around you. Going back to my example of Sudan, in 2023 when the Civil War broke out, one of my associates living in Khartoum decided to wait to evacuate. His wife's extended family did not want to leave and believed that the unrest would end quickly. Although they had the opportunity to escape on multiple foreign helicopter evacuation missions, the family decided to stay. Several days went by and the situation worsened considerably. The Army lost control of large sections of the city to the RSF, and widespread looting ran rampant. It took a considerable effort and a lot of money to safely extract him and his family all because they did not leave when it first became clear that the unrest was more than just a small disturbance. A refusal to accept the changing circumstances to our home and communities is natural. But do not let that bias force you into inaction.

What to Take With You: Go-Bag Essentials

When the time comes to evacuate, you may only have minutes to gather your belongings and leave. Preparing a "go-bag" ahead of time ensures you have the essentials you need for survival without wasting time in the moment.

1. Go-Bag Basics

A well-prepared go-bag should contain enough supplies to last for at least 72 hours. Pack it in a durable, easy-to-carry bag that can be grabbed quickly in an emergency.

- Important Documents: Include copies of your ID, insurance papers, medical records, and any legal documents. Store these In a waterproof folder.

- Cash: ATMs may not work, and digital payment methods could be unreliable during unrest. Carry enough cash to cover basic expenses for a few days.

- First Aid Kit: Pack a basic first aid kit that includes bandages, antiseptic wipes, pain relievers, any prescription medications, and a multi-tool or knife.

- Food and Water: Include non-perishable food items, like protein bars or canned goods, and enough water for at least 72 hours. A water purification method, like iodine tablets or a portable filter, is also valuable in case you run out of bottled water.

- Clothing: Pack lightweight, neutral clothing (avoid logos/flashy colors) & sturdy shoes. Don't forget warm layers & rain protection if the weather demands it.

- Portable Phone Charger: Keep a fully charged power bank or solar charger in your bag to ensure you can keep your phone operational.

- Personal Protection: If you're carrying non-lethal self-defense tools like pepper spray or a personal alarm, ensure they are packed and easily accessible.

2. Customize Based on Your Needs

Every household has different needs, so customize your go-bag accordingly. If you have children, pets, or family members with medical conditions, make sure to pack accordingly.

- Children's Needs: Pack diapers, formula, or snacks for young children. Don't forget comfort items like a favorite toy or blanket.

- Pet Supplies: If you have pets, pack food, water bowls, a leash, and any medications they need.

- Medications and Medical Supplies: If anyone in your family requires daily medication or medical equipment (such as inhalers or insulin), make sure these are prioritized.

How to Travel Safely During Unrest

Traveling during civil unrest requires a combination of careful planning, heightened awareness, and quick decision-making. Whether on foot, in a car, or using public transportation, there are specific challenges and dangers you need to prepare for. Below, we'll cover how to safely navigate each mode of transportation during an evacuation.

Traveling on Foot

Walking may be the most effective way to evacuate if roads are blocked or you live in an urban area where driving is impractical. However, moving through streets during unrest requires caution.

- Blend In and Stay Low-Profile: During civil unrest, standing out can make you a target. Dress in neutral, non-flashy clothing that doesn't associate you with any particular group or cause. Avoid wearing brightly colored clothes or political insignia that might draw unwanted attention.

- Avoid Large Crowds: Crowds can quickly become volatile during unrest, and even peaceful demonstrations can escalate into danger zones. Whenever possible, take side streets or routes away from large groups of people. Keep your distance from law enforcement lines, as confrontations can develop suddenly.

- Know Safe Locations Along Your Route: As you walk, identify potential safe havens along your route, such as open stores, office buildings, or places of worship. If the situation changes suddenly and you need to find shelter, knowing where to go can be lifesaving.

- Travel in Groups: If you're not alone, travel with others. Moving in pairs or small groups increases safety and gives you more resources to manage a situation if something unexpected happens. However, avoid large groups that might attract attention.

- Stay Vigilant: Keep your eyes and ears open for signs of changing conditions. Loud noises, shouting, or sudden movements in crowds can signal that things are escalating. Move swiftly to the nearest safe area if you sense danger.

Traveling by Car

Driving may offer faster evacuation, but it also comes with challenges like road closures, traffic, and heightened risk from protests. Being prepared to navigate these challenges can keep you safe on the road.

- Keep a Full Gas Tank: During unrest, gas stations may close, or fuel may become scarce. Always keep your vehicle's gas tank at least half full, and consider having an extra can of fuel in your car. This ensures you won't run out of gas in an area where refueling is difficult or dangerous.

- Know Your Routes: Have multiple driving routes mapped out in advance. Use smaller streets or backroads to avoid heavily trafficked areas or major city centers where unrest is likely. Avoid highways if protests are likely to block major roads.

- Drive Defensively: Be aware that during civil unrest, other drivers may act unpredictably. Be prepared to stop suddenly, change routes, or encounter dangerous driving conditions. Keep a safe distance from other vehicles, and avoid engaging with other drivers who may be agitated or aggressive.

- Stay in the Car if Safe: In many situations, staying inside your vehicle is safer than getting out, especially if the area around you is unstable. Keep your windows up and doors locked to avoid becoming vulnerable to looters or aggressive demonstrators. However, if the car is no longer a safe option (blocked in, surrounded by violent crowds), you may need to leave it and evacuate on foot.

- Emergency Supplies in the Car: Keep emergency supplies such as water, snacks, blankets, and a first aid kit in your car. If you become stranded, these can help you stay comfortable and safe until help arrives or conditions improve.

Using Public Transportation

Public transportation during civil unrest is typically not recommended due to its unpredictable nature and potential shutdowns. However, if it's your only option, there are steps you can take to stay safe.

- Monitor Service Closures: Many transit systems may reduce service or shut down entirely during periods of unrest. Check apps or websites for service updates, and have a backup plan if buses or trains become unavailable.

- Travel During Off-Peak Hours: Avoid traveling during rush hours or times when crowds are likely to be larger. Fewer people on public transport means less chance of encountering dangerous situations.

- Stay Alert: If you must use public transportation, stay alert to your surroundings. Keep an eye on fellow passengers, and sit close to the exits in case you need to leave the train or bus quickly.

- Have a Backup Plan: Know what to do if public transport becomes unavailable during your trip. Have a walking route in mind or an alternate way to reach your destination.

Coordinating with Neighbors or Local Groups for Safe Travel

During civil unrest, there's strength in numbers. Coordinating with neighbors or trusted members of your community can help ensure safer travel.

1. Establish a Network

Before unrest happens, establish a network of neighbors or local contacts who can coordinate during an evacuation. Share contact information and work out a basic plan for how you'll help each other.

- Share Evacuation Plans: If possible, coordinate with your neighbors about potential evacuation routes and meeting points. Agree to check in with one another during unrest.

2. Travel in Groups When Possible

Traveling with a group can provide additional safety. If it's safe to do so, travel with your neighbors or a small group to your destination.

- Stay Together: Don't let the group split up, as this can make people more vulnerable to danger. Stick together and communicate regularly.

Mental Preparation for Evacuation

In any crisis, mental preparation is just as important as physical readiness. During an evacuation, particularly in the midst of civil unrest, fear and panic can cloud your judgment and lead to poor decision-making. Staying mentally calm is crucial to keeping yourself and those around you safe. This section offers practical strategies for managing fear, maintaining focus, and avoiding panic during an evacuation.

1. Understanding the Impact of Stress

When faced with a high-pressure situation like an evacuation, the body's natural response is to enter fight-or-flight mode. Your adrenaline spikes, your heart races, and your ability to think clearly can become compromised. This is a normal reaction to danger, but it's important to control these feelings in order to make rational decisions.

- Recognize the Symptoms: When under extreme stress, you may experience rapid breathing, trembling, sweating, or tunnel vision. Recognizing these signs in yourself early can help you take steps to calm down before the stress escalates into panic.

- Acknowledge Your Emotions: It's normal to feel scared or anxious during an evacuation, but the key is not to let these emotions control you. Acknowledging that the situation is stressful, but that you've prepared for it, can help you stay focused and clear-headed.

2. Breathing Techniques for Calming the Mind

One of the simplest and most effective ways to manage stress during an evacuation is through controlled breathing. When your body is flooded with adrenaline, deep breathing helps lower your heart rate, stabilize your emotions, and restore mental clarity. In a previous chapter we talked about 4-4-4 box breathing.

Another simple method involves slowing down your breathing to signal to your body that you are safe. This can be done by:

- Inhaling for 4 counts.

- Exhaling for 6 counts.

The extended exhale naturally engages the parasympathetic nervous system, which helps your body calm down more quickly.

3. Stay Focused by Breaking Tasks Into Small Steps

When the situation feels overwhelming, it's easy to become paralyzed by fear. To prevent this, focus on breaking the evacuation process into small, manageable tasks. This helps keep your mind occupied and prevents panic from setting in.

- Create a Mental Checklist: Mentally walk yourself through the steps you need to take—grab your go-bag, lock the doors, ensure everyone is accounted for, start the car, and so on. By focusing on completing one task at a time, you'll feel more in control and less overwhelmed by the bigger picture.

- Prioritize Action Over Fear: Each time you check off a task, you reduce the scope of the emergency and build confidence in your ability to handle the situation. Instead of worrying about what could go wrong, focus on the immediate next step.

4. Clear and Concise Communication

Confusion during an evacuation can lead to dangerous mistakes. Keeping communication clear, concise, and calm is essential for ensuring everyone is on the same page and working together efficiently.

- Speak Clearly and Confidently: If you're communicating with others, give clear and direct instructions. Keep your voice calm, even if you feel anxious. For example, instead of saying, "I think we should leave," say, "We're leaving now. Grab your bag and head to the car."

- Avoid Overloading with Information: In a high-stress situation, people can easily become overwhelmed. Keep your instructions simple and actionable. Too much information at once can lead to confusion, so break things down into specific steps.

- Check for Understanding: If you're evacuating with family or friends, make sure everyone understands the plan. A quick confirmation—"Do you know the route we're taking?" or "Do you have your bag ready?"—helps prevent misunderstandings and keeps everyone coordinated.

5. Managing Fear and Anxiety in Others

In an evacuation, it's possible that not everyone in your group will be as calm or prepared as you are. You may need to help manage the fear or panic of family members, children, or neighbors.

- Stay Calm Yourself: People around you will take cues from your behavior. If you stay calm, they're more likely to feel secure. Use a steady, confident voice and model calm actions. This can help soothe those who are feeling more anxious.

- Offer Reassurance: Reassuring words can help reduce fear in others. Phrases like "We're prepared for this," "We have a plan," or "We're going to be safe" can ease some of the anxiety others may be feeling.

- Give Simple, Focused Instructions: In high-stress situations, some people may freeze or become indecisive. Help them by giving clear, specific tasks, such as "Help pack the bag" or "Start the car while I lock the house." This prevents them from getting stuck in panic mode.

6. Stay Flexible and Adapt to Changes

No matter how well you plan, evacuations can be unpredictable. Roadblocks, changing conditions, or unexpected hazards may require you to change course. Being mentally flexible and open to adjusting your plan is crucial.

- Accept Uncertainty: During a crisis, not everything will go according to plan. Rather than letting this cause panic, mentally prepare yourself to adapt and make decisions on the go. Flexibility is key to maintaining calm when things change unexpectedly.

- Have Backup Plans: Knowing that you have multiple routes, destinations, and plans in place can reduce anxiety. If something doesn't work out, you'll have other options to fall back on, which helps maintain a sense of control.

7. Take Short Mental Breaks

While it may seem counterintuitive during an emergency, allowing yourself short mental breaks can help you manage your stress more effectively over the course of the evacuation. Evacuations can take hours, and maintaining constant alertness can wear you down mentally.

- Pause and Breathe: Take brief moments to pause, take a few deep breaths, and clear your mind before moving on to the next task. Even a 30-second break can help reset your stress levels.

- Visualize Success: A simple visualization technique is to imagine yourself reaching your destination safely. Picture the process going smoothly, which can help shift your mindset from fear to confidence.

Evacuations can be highly stressful, but mental preparation can help you navigate these situations calmly and effectively. By managing fear, using breathing techniques, staying focused on small tasks, and communicating clearly, you can remain in control of the situation. Remember that keeping a level head and adapting as necessary is crucial to your safety during an evacuation.

In the next chapter, we will dive deeper into the importance of community coordination, where we discuss how to rely on and support those around you during times of crisis.

Final Thoughts on Evacuating Safely

Evacuation during civil unrest can be stressful, but with proper planning and situational awareness, you can reduce the risks and travel to safety. By recognizing the signs of danger, having a go-bag ready, and planning your routes carefully, you'll be better prepared to make quick, calm decisions when it matters most.

In the next chapter, we'll explore what to do if evacuation is not an option and your only recourse is to shelter in place.

7
Shelter in Place

In some cases, leaving your home during civil unrest is not an option, whether due to blocked roads, imminent danger outside, or government directives. In these situations, knowing how to effectively shelter in place becomes critical. This chapter will guide you through preparing your home for extended periods of isolation, stockpiling essential supplies, and keeping your family safe and comfortable even if utilities are disrupted. Additionally, we'll cover the importance of mental resiliency and how to start building it now—before a crisis hits.

How to Shelter in Place During Extended Unrest

Sheltering in place requires planning, calm decision-making, and the ability to adapt to changing circumstances. You may need to stay in your home for several days or longer, so it's essential to be prepared both physically and mentally.

Securing Your Home

Before you settle in for an extended period of sheltering, make sure your home is secure. This includes both physical safety measures and psychological preparedness.

- Lock All Entry Points: Double-check that all doors, windows, and garage doors are securely locked. If you have window bars or shutters, close them to deter intruders and protect against stray objects or debris.

- Create Layers of Security: Use door braces, dowels in window tracks, and any other reinforcements to make it more difficult for outsiders to enter. Even simple security measures can increase your peace of mind during unrest.

- Block Out Windows: Consider covering windows with thick curtains or blackout material to prevent anyone from seeing inside. Not only does this help with security, but it also gives a sense of privacy and calm within your home.

Stockpiling Essentials to Last Several Days

When you shelter in place, you need to ensure you have enough supplies to sustain yourself and your family for at least several days, if not longer. It's important to stockpile without panic buying—focus on practical needs rather than excessive hoarding.

1. Food and Water

- Non-Perishable Food: Stock up on canned goods, dried fruits, nuts, pasta, rice, and other long-lasting foods. Focus on items that are easy to prepare and require minimal water or electricity if those utilities are unavailable.

- Water: Each person in your household needs at least one gallon of water per day for drinking and sanitation. Have enough bottled water on hand for several days. If you have pets, remember to stock water for them as well. If storing large quantities of bottled water is impractical, consider investing in a water filtration system or purification tablets.

2. Medications and First Aid

- Prescription Medications: Ensure that anyone in your household who relies on daily medications has enough to last through an extended period of unrest. If possible, keep an extra supply on hand for emergencies.

- First Aid Kit: Your first aid kit should include basic supplies like bandages, antiseptic, pain relievers, and any necessary medical equipment (e.g., inhalers, insulin, etc.).

- Expiration Dates: Keep an eye on expiration dates for medicines and first aid supplies. Having extra on hand is great but make sure you are using the oldest stock first so that whatever you have on hand is the freshest available. Putting something in a box only to pull it out when you need it five years later to find it is well past its expiration date would be disheartening to say the least.

3. Hygiene and Sanitation Supplies

Toiletries: Stock up on toilet paper, soap, hand sanitizer, and feminine hygiene products. If water is limited, dry shampoo and body wipes can help maintain personal cleanliness. Maintaining good hygiene during a crisis is important as it helps provide a sense of mental stability and security in addition to the obvious health benefits.

Trash Bags: In case of extended periods without garbage collection, trash bags and sealable containers can help manage waste and prevent health hazards.

4. Power and Light

- Flashlights and Batteries: Keep flashlights, lanterns,

and extra batteries in an easily accessible location. Solar-powered or crank-charged devices can be invaluable if the power is out for an extended period.

- Backup Power Source: If possible, consider having a backup power source, such as a portable generator or battery banks to keep essential electronics, like phones and radios, charged.

Staying Safe and Comfortable if the Power or Water Is Cut Off

Civil unrest can lead to disruptions in utilities, including power, water, and gas. Preparing for these outages ensures you stay safe and as comfortable as possible until the situation stabilizes.

1. Staying Warm or Cool

- Temperature Control: Depending on the season, staying warm or cool may become a challenge. If you lose power in the winter, layering clothing and using heavy blankets will help retain body heat. If it's summer, close blinds or curtains to block sunlight and keep the home cooler. Using blankets in between rooms without doors can help conserve heat in smaller areas.

- Alternative Heating or Cooling: If it's winter, and you have a fireplace, make sure you have a supply of firewood. In the summer, battery-powered fans can provide relief, and staying hydrated is essential for regulating body temperature.

2. Safe Cooking

- Gas Stoves or Camping Stoves: If the power goes out, a gas stove (if available) or a camping stove can be useful for preparing hot meals. Just be sure to use them in a well-ventilated area to avoid carbon monoxide buildup.

- Cold Meals: Have non-perishable, ready-to-eat foods that don't require cooking in case utilities are out for an extended time.

3. Water Conservation and Safety

If water services are disrupted, you'll need to conserve water and ensure it's safe for use.

- Water Purification: If you run out of bottled water, having water purification tablets or a filtration system allows you to safely drink from alternate sources like rainwater. There are also water purification disinfectant systems that don't use chemicals or require electricity that can kill viruses and bacteria on contact. Clairify Quantum Disinfectant is one example of this technology that could be useful if access to power and clean water is lost.

- Conserving Water: Use water only for essential activities like drinking and sanitation. Avoid unnecessary water use for tasks like cleaning unless absolutely necessary.

Communication and Keeping Morale Up with Family Members

Sheltering in place, especially for an extended time, can lead to anxiety, boredom, and frayed tempers. Keeping lines of communication open and finding ways to keep morale up are critical to ensuring everyone's well-being.

1. Establish a Routine

Having a daily routine provides structure and stability during uncertain times.

- Create Schedules: Develop a simple daily schedule that includes tasks like preparing meals, cleaning, and relaxation time. Routines help break up the day and provide a sense of normalcy.

- Rotate Responsibilities: Give family members specific roles or responsibilities. This not only keeps everyone occupied but also fosters a sense of teamwork and shared purpose.

2. Stay Connected

If the internet or cell service is still available, use it to stay connected with loved ones and the outside world.

- Check in Regularly: Schedule regular check-ins with friends or family who live elsewhere. This not only provides reassurance but also helps everyone feel connected and supported.

- Entertainment: Don't overlook the importance of having entertainment options. Books, board games, or other offline activities can help pass the time and distract from the stress of the situation.

3. Keep Communication Clear

Clear and calm communication is key to maintaining peace in the household during a crisis. When stress levels rise, misunderstandings are more likely.

- Talk Openly: Encourage open dialogue about how everyone is feeling. Acknowledge the stress but focus on the steps you're taking to stay safe.

- Reassure Children: If you have children, explain the situation in a way that's honest but not overly frightening. Reassure them that you have a plan and that they are safe.

Knowing When to Reassess the Situation and Make New Decisions

Even if you're sheltering in place, you must continually reassess the situation to determine if it's still safe to stay or if you need to leave. Be aware of changing circumstances and new information.

1. Monitor the Situation

Keep yourself informed about what's happening in your area, even while sheltering.

- Use Multiple Sources: Rely on several trusted sources, including news outlets, police scanners, or local government updates. Misinformation can spread easily during a crisis, so verify what you hear before making any major decisions.

- Stay Alert to Changing Conditions: Are the protests or unrest growing closer? Are utility disruptions worsening? Has law enforcement lost control of the area? If conditions are deteriorating, you may need to consider evacuation options.

2. Reevaluate Your Safety

Periodically check whether your home remains the safest option.

- Evaluate Your Supplies: Are your food, water, and medication supplies running low? Are you running out of fuel or battery power? If your resources are dwindling, it might be time to find a safer place to go.

- Reassess the Risk: If the situation outside stabilizes, you might not need to leave your home. However, if violence or danger increases, you should be ready to make an informed decision about evacuation.

Building Mental Resiliency Now

Mental resilience is crucial in any crisis, especially during long periods of isolation or uncertainty. Rather than waiting for a crisis to occur, begin building your mental strength now, so you're better prepared when the time comes.

1. Practice Self-Control Daily

- Delay Gratification: One way to strengthen self-control is by practicing small acts of discipline, such as delaying a treat or setting goals and achieving them step by step. This builds your mental endurance for more significant challenges in the future.

- Mindfulness: Incorporating mindfulness practices, such as meditation or focused breathing, can help you stay calm under pressure. This makes it easier to control emotions and stress when you're faced with a crisis.

2. Exposure to Controlled Stress

Gradual exposure to controlled stressors helps build resilience, making it easier to handle real crises.

- Take on New Challenges: Push yourself to tackle new, challenging tasks in your daily life—whether it's learning a new skill, facing a fear, or overcoming a physical obstacle. These small victories build the mental toughness needed in high-stress situations.

- Cold Showers or Physical Challenges: Subjecting yourself to brief periods of physical discomfort, such as cold showers or strenuous exercise, can train your body and mind to adapt to stressful conditions.

3. Practice Positive Self-Talk

The way you talk to yourself during stressful times has a powerful impact on your ability to stay calm and focused.

- Reframe Negative Thoughts: When faced with a challenging situation, practice reframing negative thoughts. Instead of saying, *"I can't handle this,"* try saying, *"This is hard, but I can manage it."*

- Build Confidence Through Action: By gradually

exposing yourself to manageable challenges, you'll build confidence in your ability to handle larger crises.

Staying Mentally Engaged: The Role of Entertainment

Sheltering in place for an extended period can lead to boredom and frustration, especially if you're cut off from regular activities, work, or entertainment options. Having a supply of non-electronic entertainment can make a significant difference in maintaining morale and reducing stress. Keeping your mind occupied helps to alleviate anxiety and provides a much-needed mental break from the stress of the situation.

1. Books and Reading Materials

- Stock Up on Books: Whether it's novels, non-fiction, or magazines, having a variety of reading materials on hand can be a great way to pass the time. Books also provide an escape from the immediate reality and can offer inspiration or new perspectives.

- Educational Materials: You can also use the time to learn something new. Stock up on books related to skills you've always wanted to learn, whether it's gardening, home repair, or even basic survival techniques.

2. Board Games and Card Games

- Classic Board Games: Games like chess, checkers, Scrabble, and Monopoly are not only great for passing the time but also for keeping the mind sharp and promoting family bonding.

- Deck of Cards: A simple deck of cards provides endless entertainment with games like Solitaire, Rummy, Poker, and Go Fish. Card games are versatile and require minimal space and setup.

- Puzzle Games: Jigsaw puzzles or brain-teaser puzzles like Sudoku or crossword books offer solo or group entertainment and help engage the mind, reducing feelings of restlessness.

3. Arts and Crafts

- Drawing and Coloring: Stock up on sketchpads, pencils, or coloring books, especially if you have children. Art can be a calming activity that helps to channel stress creatively.

- Craft Supplies: If you or your family members enjoy knitting, sewing, or other crafts, having a stash of supplies can keep your hands busy and provide a sense of accomplishment.

4. Low-Tech Pastimes

- Writing or Journaling: Encourage journaling or creative writing. Not only is this a therapeutic outlet for stress, but it's also a way to document the experience and reflect on the emotions you're going through.

- Music and Singing: If you have acoustic instruments like a guitar or harmonica, playing music can be an uplifting way to pass the time. Singing together, even without instruments, can help reduce stress and foster a sense of togetherness.

- Storytelling: For families or groups, sharing stories—whether fictional or personal—can create bonds and provide distraction from the situation. This can be particularly effective with children who may need additional reassurance during uncertain times.

5. Physical Activities Indoors

- Bodyweight Exercises: While exercise may seem like a less obvious form of entertainment, it can reduce stress and improve mental health. Simple activities like stretching, yoga, or bodyweight exercises don't require equipment and can help release endorphins to improve mood.

- Games with Limited Space: Even in a small living area, you can still engage in fun activities. For example, games like charades, hide-and-seek for kids, or modified versions of sports can help break up the day and encourage movement.

6. Rotating Entertainment Options

- Variety is Key: Don't rely on one form of entertainment. Rotate activities throughout the day to keep things fresh. For example, start the day with some reading, then move to a board game in the afternoon, and perhaps journal or sketch in the evening.

- Involve Everyone: Let each family member take turns choosing an activity to promote engagement and give everyone something to look forward to.

7. Unplug from Digital Entertainment

While it may be tempting to rely on smartphones,

tablets, or TVs for entertainment, especially if power and internet are still available, it's important to balance screen time with more active or creative activities. Too much time on digital devices can lead to mental fatigue or heighten anxiety, especially when continuously consuming news about the crisis.

The Importance of Staying Engaged

Having a range of entertainment options during shelter-in-place periods not only alleviates boredom but also reduces stress and helps maintain mental well-being. Keeping busy with enjoyable activities provides much-needed distraction, enhances family bonds, and offers small moments of joy in an otherwise challenging time. Preparing these resources in advance ensures that when the time comes, you'll be able to stay occupied and positive throughout the duration of the shelter-in-place order.

Conclusion

Sheltering in place during civil unrest can be challenging, but with the right preparations, it doesn't have to feel overwhelming. Focus on creating a secure, comfortable environment, stockpiling essentials, and staying connected with loved ones. Mental resilience is just as important as physical preparation, so start building your inner strength now to ensure you can handle any crisis with confidence.

The information provided in the following chapter is for educational and informational purposes only and is not intended as a substitute for professional medical advice, diagnosis, or treatment. The author is not a licensed healthcare provider, and the medical tips shared in this chapter should not be considered a replacement for consulting with qualified medical professionals. In the event of an emergency or a serious health issue, always seek immediate assistance from a licensed healthcare provider or emergency services.

By reading this chapter, you acknowledge that health situations can vary, and it is important to consult with a medical professional before acting on any advice provided here. The author and publisher are not responsible for any adverse effects or consequences that may result from the use of information provided in this chapter. Always prioritize professional medical guidance over any general recommendations provided here.

8
Handling Health Emergencies

During civil unrest, access to medical care can be severely limited, making it crucial for you to manage health emergencies independently, at least for a short period. This chapter covers the essentials of first aid, chronic health management, and strategies to ensure that you and your loved ones stay healthy when traditional medical services may not be easily available. Knowing how to handle medical situations during a crisis can reduce stress and potentially save lives.

Basic First Aid for Common Injuries During Civil Unrest

Civil unrest situations can sometimes lead to physical injury, whether from accidents, broken glass, or direct confrontations. Learning basic first aid is essential for handling common injuries when professional medical help may be delayed or unavailable. Here are some of the most important first aid techniques you should know:

1. Treating Cuts and Lacerations

- Stop the Bleeding: Apply direct pressure to the wound using a clean cloth, bandage, or gauze. If the bleeding doesn't stop after 10 minutes, continue applying pressure and elevate the injury if possible.

- Clean the Wound: Once the bleeding is under control, wash the wound with clean water to remove debris. Avoid using hydrogen peroxide or alcohol as these can damage tissue—mild soap and water are sufficient.

- Apply a Bandage: Cover the wound with a sterile bandage or clean cloth. While older advice recommended letting wounds "breathe," the current medical consensus is that keeping the wound covered and moist actually promotes faster healing and reduces the risk of infection. A covered wound helps maintain a more hydrated environment, preventing scabbing and minimizing scarring. It's important to change the dressing daily or whenever it becomes wet or dirty to keep the area clean and free from bacteria. This approach leads to better healing outcomes than leaving a wound exposed to air.

- Monitor for Infection: Watch for signs of infection, such as redness, swelling, pus, or increased pain. If you suspect infection, apply a double or triple antibiotic ointment, such as Neosporin, if available. This can help prevent bacterial growth and support healing. However, if symptoms worsen or persist, seek medical care as soon as possible.

2. Treating Burns

Burns are another common injury, whether from cooking, accidents, or fire hazards during unrest.

First-Degree Burns: A mild burn affecting only the outer layer of skin (epidermis). It causes redness, pain, and minor swelling, but no blisters. An example is a typical sunburn.

Cool the burn with cold water or a cold, damp cloth. Avoid ice as it can damage the skin further. Apply aloe vera or burn ointment and cover with a sterile bandage if necessary.

Second-Degree Burns: A burn that affects both the outer layer of skin (epidermis) and the underlying layer (dermis). It causes pain, redness, swelling, and blisters. The skin may appear wet or shiny.

These burns will have blisters. Avoid popping blisters, as this increases the risk of infection. Cool the burn as you would a first-degree burn and cover it with a non-stick bandage. Seek medical attention if the burn covers a large area or looks severe.

Third-Degree Burns: A severe burn that penetrates all layers of the skin, potentially damaging underlying tissues. The burn area may appear white, charred, or leathery, and sensation may be lost due to nerve damage. Immediate medical attention is required.

These burns require immediate medical attention. They will be white, charred, or leathery in appearance. Do not apply water or any ointment; instead, cover the burn with a sterile cloth and seek emergency care immediately.

3. Treating Sprains and Fractures

- Rest: If you suspect a sprain or fracture, have the injured person stop using the affected limb.

- Ice: Apply a cold compress to reduce swelling and numb the area, but ice should never be applied directly to the skin, as it can cause frostbite or skin damage. Instead, wrap the ice or an ice pack in a cloth or towel and apply it to the affected area for 15-20 minutes at a time. Allow the skin to rest for 20-30 minutes before reapplying if needed. This helps reduce inflammation without causing harm to the skin.

- Compression: Wrap the injury with a bandage to provide support and reduce swelling. The bandage should be snug but not too tight, as excessive pressure can restrict blood flow and cause further damage. You should be able to insert a finger under the bandage comfortably. If the area becomes numb, cold, or changes color, loosen the bandage immediately. Be sure to rewrap if the compression becomes too loose.

- Elevation: Keep the injured limb elevated above the heart if possible to help control swelling.

- Fractures: If you suspect a broken bone, immobilize the limb using a makeshift splint to prevent further injury. You can create a splint using common household items such as a rolled-up magazine, a sturdy stick, or a straight piece of cardboard. Secure the splint to the limb with cloth strips, tape, or a belt, making sure it's snug but not too tight to avoid cutting off circulation. The goal is to keep the limb as still and stable as possible. Seek medical care as soon as possible, but keeping the limb immobilized until help arrives will help minimize damage.

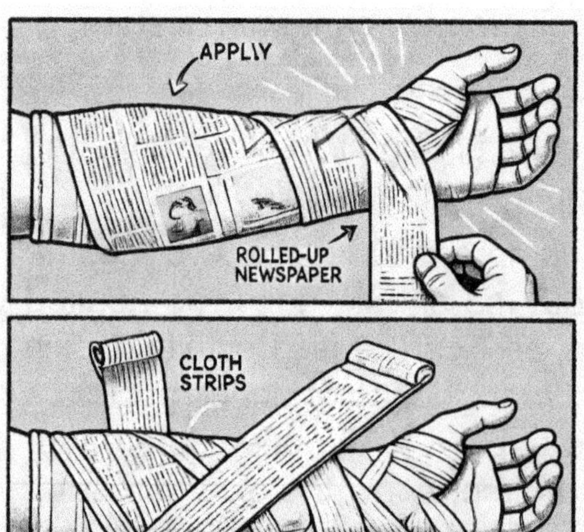

4. Treating Eye Injuries

Eye injuries can occur from flying debris or exposure to chemicals.

- Flushing the Eye: For chemical exposure or debris, gently flush the eye with clean water for at least 15 minutes. Avoid rubbing the eye. At home eye wash stations with saline solutions are available to have on hand if this is a potential concern due to the environment in which you live but running clean tap water over the eye works as well.

- If a Foreign Object Is Lodged in or Near the Eye: Do not attempt to remove a foreign object that is lodged in or near the eye. Doing so can cause further injury. Instead, protect the eye by covering it gently with a clean cloth, sterile bandage, or eye shield, ensuring the object is not disturbed. Seek immediate professional medical help.

- **Seek Professional Help**: Eye injuries should be treated by a professional as soon as possible to avoid long-term damage. Use an eye patch or clean cloth to cover the eye until you can get help.

Accessing Medical Care When Hospitals and Emergency Services Are Overwhelmed

During times of civil unrest, hospitals and emergency services may be overwhelmed with an influx of patients. It's important to understand how to access care when resources are limited and know alternative options if traditional routes are unavailable. When traveling to and from a location for medical care, ensure your safety by following the advice given in the chapter on Personal Safety on the Streets.

1. Know Your Local Urgent Care Centers

Urgent care centers are often less overwhelmed than hospitals during a crisis and can be an alternative for non-life-threatening emergencies. Find out where the nearest centers are located and keep their contact information handy. It's also wise to know their hours of operation and whether they have extended hours during emergencies.

2. Telemedicine and Virtual Consultations

If the roads are unsafe or hospitals are too crowded, telemedicine can be a lifesaver. Many healthcare providers offer virtual consultations where you can speak with a doctor over the phone or video call. They can provide advice on how to manage certain conditions and may be able to prescribe medications remotely.

- How to Access Telemedicine: Have your doctor's or healthcare provider's telemedicine options ready before an emergency. Apps like Teladoc, MDLIVE, or services offered through your health insurance provider can connect you with a medical professional without having to leave your home.

3. Home Remedies for Minor Illnesses

In situations where medical care is delayed, you may have to rely on home remedies to manage minor illnesses. Some basic remedies include:

- Fever: Use over-the-counter fever reducers like ibuprofen or acetaminophen, if available. If not, sponge baths with lukewarm water can help lower body temperature.

- Cough and Sore Throat: Honey and lemon in warm water can soothe a sore throat. Gargling with saltwater also helps reduce inflammation.

- Diarrhea and Dehydration: Stay hydrated by

drinking water mixed with a little salt and sugar (homemade oral rehydration solution) to replace lost electrolytes.

4. Emergency First Aid Classes

Take a first aid or CPR class ahead of time. Many organizations, such as the Red Cross, offer in-person and online classes that can equip you with the skills necessary to manage health emergencies when help is not immediately available. Many local health departments also offer classes to the public.

Keeping Essential Medications Stocked and Finding Alternatives in Emergencies

Managing chronic illnesses or conditions that require regular medication can be difficult during a crisis. Ensuring you have enough of your prescribed medications on hand and knowing alternatives if you run out is critical to managing your health.

1. Build a Medication Stockpile

- Request Extra Prescriptions: Talk to your doctor about getting a longer-term prescription, especially if you rely on daily medication. Some insurance providers may allow you to fill a 90-day supply instead of a 30-day supply.

- Store Medications Properly: Keep medications in a cool, dry place and check expiration dates regularly. If possible, rotate your stock so that you're always using the oldest supply first.

- Keep a List of Medications: Maintain a list of all medications you and your family members take, including dosage instructions. Keep this list in your go-bag and on your person during emergencies in case you need to seek a refill from a different pharmacy or a relief station.

2. Finding Alternatives in an Emergency

If your medication runs out and pharmacies are closed, you may need to find temporary alternatives or ways to manage your condition until medical care is accessible again.

- Over-the-Counter Substitutes: Some prescription medications have over-the-counter alternatives that can help in the short term. For example, ibuprofen can be a temporary substitute for certain pain medications, and antihistamines like Benadryl can help with allergic reactions or minor asthma symptoms.

- Natural Alternatives: Some herbal remedies may offer relief in the absence of traditional medications. For example, ginger and peppermint can help with nausea, while turmeric and willow bark are known for their anti-inflammatory properties. Be cautious when using herbal alternatives, and research their proper usage and any interactions they may have with other medications.

Dealing with Chronic Health Issues When Supplies Are Limited

Managing chronic health conditions during a crisis can be one of the most stressful aspects of civil unrest, especially if you can't access necessary medications or treatments. Here are some strategies to manage common chronic conditions in emergencies.

1. Diabetes Management

For those with diabetes, access to insulin and glucose monitoring tools is essential.

- Stockpile Insulin and Supplies: Work with your

healthcare provider to build a stockpile of insulin and other supplies, such as test strips and syringes. Insulin should be stored in the refrigerator, but it can remain at room temperature for up to 28 days if necessary.

- Alternative Blood Sugar Management: If you run out of supplies, be extra vigilant about your diet. Avoid processed sugars, carbohydrates, and alcohol to keep your blood sugar levels stable until you can access proper care.

2. Asthma and Respiratory Conditions

People with asthma or other respiratory conditions rely on inhalers or nebulizers to manage their symptoms.

- Stock Inhalers: Request an extra inhaler from your doctor or pharmacy in case of an emergency.

- Minimizing Triggers: During unrest, the air quality might worsen due to smoke from fires or tear gas used by law enforcement. Keep windows closed, stay indoors as much as possible, and use a mask to filter air if needed. If you have a nebulizer, make sure it's in good working condition and have a backup power source if electricity is unreliable.

3. Heart Disease

Managing heart disease during a crisis requires vigilance to avoid complications.

- Keep a Supply of Medication: Make sure you have enough blood pressure medications, blood thinners, or cholesterol-lowering drugs. Have a plan for refills or alternatives if supplies run low.

- Diet and Exercise: Stress during unrest can elevate blood pressure. Practice stress-relief techniques and avoid high-sodium or high-fat foods to keep your heart healthy.

Mental Health During Extended Crises

Prolonged periods of stress and uncertainty can exacerbate mental health conditions or lead to new challenges. Managing mental health is just as important as physical health, especially during extended civil unrest.

1. Recognizing Signs of Anxiety and Depression

- Anxiety: Feelings of fear, restlessness, rapid breathing, and a racing heart are common during high-stress situations. It's important to manage these symptoms before they escalate.

- Depression: If you or a loved one starts experiencing prolonged sadness, loss of interest in daily activities, or feelings of hopelessness, it may be a sign of depression. Seek professional help through telemedicine if available or engage in activities that provide a sense of normalcy and accomplishment.

2. Daily Techniques to Stay Mentally Strong

- Routine: Maintaining a daily routine helps provide structure and reduces feelings of chaos. Even simple routines, like making breakfast or doing a light workout, can help.

- Mindfulness and Meditation: Breathing exercises, mindfulness techniques, or meditation can help reduce stress. Spending just 10 minutes a day focusing on your breathing can lower your stress levels and help you stay calm.

- Talking with Loved Ones: Open communication about how you're feeling is important. Sharing your concerns with a trusted friend or family member can help you process your emotions and feel less isolated.

Taking Control of Your Health in a Crisis

During civil unrest, access to medical care may be limited, but by preparing ahead of time, you can manage many health emergencies independently. Stockpiling essential medications, knowing basic first aid, and understanding how to manage chronic conditions will help you navigate a crisis safely. Staying mentally resilient and practicing daily stress-relief techniques is crucial for maintaining your overall health during an extended emergency.

In the next chapter, we'll cover community collaboration—how to rely on neighbors and build local support networks during and after times of crisis.

9
Rebuilding After the Unrest

In the aftermath of civil unrest, it's normal to feel a sense of relief mixed with uncertainty. The crisis may have passed, but the transition back to a safer environment can bring new challenges. Rebuilding your life, community, and sense of security after unrest requires patience, communication, and careful planning. In this chapter, we'll explore how to rely on your neighbors, reconnect with your community, and make long-term plans to strengthen your resilience for the future.

Relying on Neighbors During a Crisis and Beyond

During any crisis, communities that work together are often the ones that survive and recover the quickest. Reaching out to your neighbors, sharing resources, and pooling knowledge during the unrest can make the experience more bearable, but the strength of these relationships also becomes invaluable when the time comes to rebuild.

1.   Strength in Numbers

- Pooling Resources: During a crisis, pooling resources like food, water, tools, or medical supplies with your neighbors can help everyone get through the worst. After the unrest subsides, these shared efforts create a stronger sense of unity and make rebuilding easier.

- Skills Exchange: Each member of your community likely has different skills—some may be skilled in repairs, others in gardening, and some might have medical or technical expertise. Leveraging these collective talents will not only make the rebuilding process more efficient but will also foster a sense of camaraderie and shared purpose.

2. Building Mutual Support Systems

- Developing a Neighborhood Watch: After the unrest, neighbors should come together to discuss how to better support each other in the future. Setting up a neighborhood watch or a mutual aid network can improve security and resilience, reducing the fear of future unrest.

- Communication Channels: Maintain regular communication with your neighbors, even when things return to normal. A group messaging app or a neighborhood social media page can serve as a way to quickly disseminate information and alert others of any new potential threats.

3. Supporting Vulnerable Neighbors

- Helping the Elderly or Disabled: Not everyone in your community may be able to rebuild on their own. Offering assistance to elderly or disabled neighbors can ensure that everyone recovers and rebuilds as a collective.

- Childcare and Emotional Support: During and after crises, families with children may need extra support. Offering help with childcare or just providing a listening ear can make a big difference as families adjust to a new reality.

Returning to a Sense of Normalcy

The return to normal life after unrest can be gradual and complicated. You may find that daily routines, local infrastructure, or community relationships have been disrupted. The goal is to reestablish your sense of security and stability while allowing yourself and others time to process the emotional impact of what has happened.

1.   Start with Simple Routines

- Gradual Return to Routine: Resuming small, daily tasks—like morning walks, family meals, or work routines—can help create a sense of normalcy. These activities signal to your mind that the crisis is over and help you regain a sense of control.

- Reengage with Work or School: Returning to your workplace or sending children back to school may seem daunting after an upheaval, but it's an important step in moving forward. Employers and schools may also provide resources to help you cope with the transition.

2.   Emotional Recovery Takes Time

- Be Patient with Yourself: Emotional recovery may take time, and it's normal to feel anxious or uncertain even after the unrest has passed. Give yourself permission to process these emotions and seek support when needed.

- Talk to Others: Talking through your experience with friends, family, or even a counselor can help you cope with the stress or trauma caused by the unrest. Sharing your story allows you to externalize your feelings and gain perspective.

Reassessing Safety and Making Long-Term Improvements

After the crisis has passed and life begins to stabilize, it's important to reassess your safety measures and make any necessary long-term improvements to your preparedness plan. This includes evaluating what worked, what didn't, and what steps you can take to protect yourself and your loved ones in the future.

1. Evaluate What Went Well

    • Strengths in Your Plan: Look back at what aspects of your emergency plan worked during the unrest. Did you have enough supplies? Were your evacuation routes viable? Did your communication plan work smoothly? Identifying these strengths will help you maintain a solid foundation for future planning.

2. Identify Areas for Improvement

    • Weaknesses and Adjustments: It's equally important to acknowledge what didn't go as planned. Did you run out of key supplies? Was there a breakdown in communication with family members? Make adjustments based on these gaps and consider new tools, supplies, or strategies to strengthen your preparedness.

3. Consider Long-Term Upgrades

    • Home Security Improvements: After unrest, you may want to invest in stronger security measures. Consider upgrading to a more comprehensive home security system, adding reinforced windows or doors, or even installing motion-sensing lights and cameras.

    • Stockpiling Essentials: If you found that your stockpile ran out too quickly, consider increasing the amount of food, water, and other essentials you store. Creating a system of rotating supplies can ensure that you always have fresh resources on hand.

4.   Build Relationships with Local Authorities

- Engage with Local Officials: After unrest, local government and law enforcement agencies often reassess their community strategies. Take this time to connect with local officials, attend community meetings, and stay informed about public safety initiatives.

- Participate in Safety Drills: If local emergency services offer safety drills or workshops, participate in them. It's an excellent way to stay prepared and gain insights into community-level response efforts.

How to Talk to Children and Family Members About What Happened

One of the most challenging aspects of recovering from a crisis is explaining it to children and family members who may have been affected by the unrest. Having honest and age-appropriate conversations can help them process what happened and reassure them that they are now safe.

1.   Start with Reassurance

- Address Their Fears: Children, in particular, may still feel scared or anxious after unrest, even if the immediate danger has passed. Start by reassuring them that they are now safe and that you're there to protect them.

- Be Honest but Gentle: While you want to reassure your family, it's also important to be honest about what happened. Tailor the explanation based on their age and emotional maturity. For younger children, you might simply explain that there was a lot of commotion but that everything is calm now. For older kids, you may want to discuss the reasons behind the unrest more thoroughly.

2.   Encourage Questions

- Open Communication: Encourage your family members to ask questions about what happened. Let them know it's okay to be scared or confused. Answer their questions as clearly and calmly as you can.

- Validate Their Emotions: Let children and family members know that their feelings are valid. Whether they feel scared, angry, or anxious, it's important to acknowledge their emotions and remind them that these feelings will pass with time.

3.   Rebuild a Sense of Security

- Focus on Positive Actions: Talk about the steps you took to keep them safe and the things you will continue to do in the future to protect them. Involving children in small, manageable tasks, like restocking supplies, can give them a sense of control and confidence.

- Create New Routines: Creating new, comforting routines can help children feel grounded. Even small rituals, like bedtime stories or regular family meals, can go a long way in reestablishing a sense of safety.

Reconnecting with Your Community and Supporting Each Other

After unrest subsides, communities often come together to rebuild, heal, and support one another. Reconnecting with neighbors and local groups can provide emotional support and help restore a sense of normalcy. Working together with your community makes everyone stronger and more resilient in the face of future challenges.

1.   Community Rebuilding Initiatives

- Get Involved: Many communities organize clean-up efforts or neighborhood watch programs after unrest. Volunteering for these initiatives not only helps restore your surroundings but also strengthens bonds with neighbors.

- Support Local Businesses: If local shops or businesses were affected by the unrest, supporting them as they rebuild is vital to helping the community recover economically. Small gestures like shopping locally or participating in fundraising events can make a significant difference.

2.   Share Your Knowledge

- Offer Your Skills: Whether it's helping with repairs, organizing food drives, or simply offering a helping hand to those in need, sharing your skills with the community helps build collective resilience.

- Teach Preparedness: If you feel confident in your emergency planning, share what you've learned with your neighbors. Organizing community preparedness workshops can help others learn from your experience and ensure that everyone is more prepared for future crises.

Returning to Normal: Examples of Community Recovery After Crisis

Communities around the world have faced various crises throughout history, and their ability to return to a sense of normalcy and rebuild stronger often serves as a source of hope and inspiration. While each crisis presents its own challenges, many communities have demonstrated remarkable resilience, pulling together to heal and rebuild. Below are a few examples of how communities came together after a major crisis, and what we can learn from them.

1.   The COVID-19 Pandemic (2020–2022)

The COVID-19 pandemic was one of the most significant global crises in modern history, disrupting daily life, collapsing economies, and causing widespread illness and death. However, in the face of lockdowns, social isolation, and overwhelmed healthcare systems, communities adapted, rebuilt, and reconnected.

- Community Resilience: During the pandemic, local communities formed mutual aid networks to support vulnerable populations. Neighbors checked in on each other, shared resources like food and hygiene products, and organized online groups to coordinate help for those in need. These grassroots efforts not only provided immediate relief but also strengthened bonds within communities.

- Embracing New Normals: As vaccines became available and restrictions eased, communities worked to return to normal life while adapting to new realities. Workplaces introduced hybrid models, schools reopened with enhanced safety protocols, and businesses slowly resumed operations. The pandemic pushed societies to rethink healthcare, mental health support, and digital connectivity.

- Key Takeaway: The pandemic showed that even in isolation, communities can find ways to support each other. Whether through virtual check-ins, sharing supplies, or reimagining how to gather safely, people came together to weather the storm.

As life returned to normal, the lessons learned from community cooperation laid the foundation for greater resilience in future crises.

2.   Hurricane Katrina (2005, United States)

Hurricane Katrina devastated New Orleans and the Gulf Coast in August 2005, causing widespread destruction, displacing over a million people, and resulting in nearly 2,000 deaths. The aftermath left the city's infrastructure crippled, and the slow governmental response further compounded the crisis. However, despite the immense tragedy, the city and its residents embarked on a long and arduous journey of recovery and rebuilding.

- Grassroots Rebuilding: In the wake of government delays, community groups, volunteers, and residents took the lead in recovery efforts. Neighborhood organizations like the Common Ground Collective and local churches became hubs for distributing food, water, and medical care. Volunteers from across the country came to help rebuild homes, while residents banded together to restore their neighborhoods, block by block.

- Resilient Spirit: The city's cultural heritage, particularly its deep-rooted music and arts community, played a vital role in healing and recovery. Musicians, artists, and performers returned to the city to help reignite the spirit of New Orleans. Street parades, jazz clubs, and festivals like Mardi Gras slowly returned, signaling the city's resilience and determination to overcome the devastation.

- Key Takeaway: The recovery from Hurricane Katrina was a testament to the power of community action in the face of slow institutional support. Residents relied on each other to rebuild homes, restore services, and revive the city's cultural heart. The rebuilding process was long and difficult, but it demonstrated that community solidarity can drive recovery even after large-scale disasters.

3.   The Christchurch Earthquake (2011, New Zealand)

In February 2011, Christchurch, New Zealand, was struck by a devastating earthquake that killed 185 people and severely damaged much of the city's infrastructure. With buildings crumbling and essential services interrupted, the recovery process was complex and prolonged. However, the people of Christchurch banded together to rebuild their city, demonstrating resilience and community spirit.

- Community-Led Recovery: In the immediate aftermath of the earthquake, local residents took matters into their own hands. The Student Volunteer Army, a group of university students, mobilized thousands of volunteers to help clear debris, deliver supplies, and assist affected residents. This grassroots effort played a crucial role in the early recovery, filling gaps left by official relief agencies.

- Reshaping the City: The rebuilding of Christchurch has been a long-term effort that involved not only restoring the city's infrastructure but also reimagining it. Community consultations and involvement were key to redesigning public spaces and infrastructure. This rebuilding effort focused on making the city more resilient to future disasters while preserving its unique character.

- Key Takeaway: The recovery of Christchurch highlighted the importance of local initiative and grassroots involvement. By embracing community-led recovery efforts and actively participating in the rebuilding process, the residents of Christchurch were able to turn a disaster into an opportunity for positive change and urban renewal.

Final Thoughts on Rebuilding After Unrest

Rebuilding after civil unrest is a process that takes time, cooperation, and careful planning. By relying on your neighbors, reassessing your safety strategies, and supporting your community, you can help create a stronger, more resilient environment for the future. Taking the lessons learned from the crisis and applying them to your long-term plans will help you feel more confident and secure in the face of potential future unrest.

In the next chapter, we will focus on rebuilding emotional and mental resilience after the trauma of civil unrest, offering tips on processing fear and grief while moving forward.

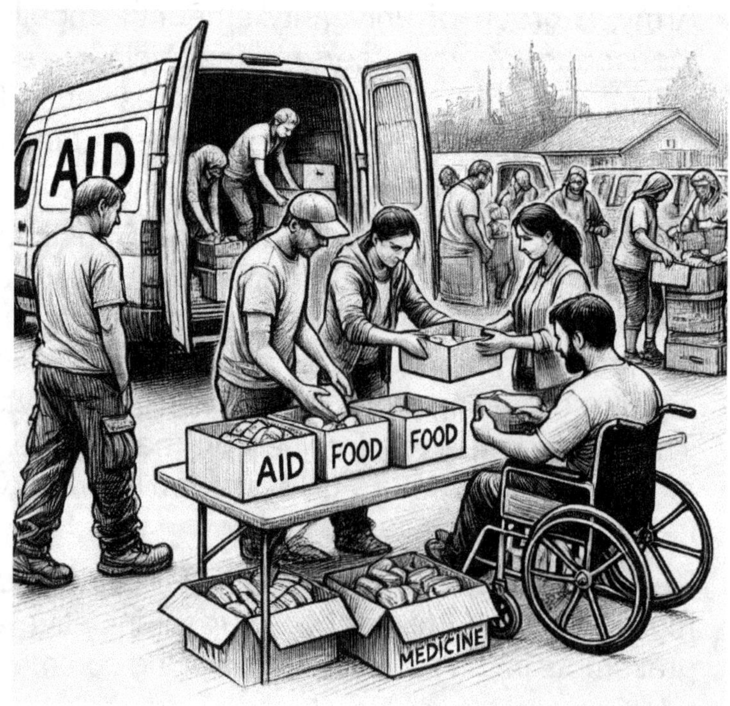

10
Staying Resilient in Uncertain Times

In a world where uncertainty and instability can emerge at any moment, staying resilient and prepared is no longer a choice—it's a necessity. Throughout this guide, we've explored the practical steps and mental strategies that can help you navigate civil unrest, protect your loved ones, and rebuild after a crisis. Now, as we reach the conclusion of this journey, it's time to reflect on the key takeaways that will empower you to face future challenges with confidence and determination.

Understanding and Accepting Fear

It's important to recognize that fear is a natural and justified response to the unpredictable challenges we face today. Whether it's civil unrest, natural disasters, or societal breakdown, it's completely understandable to feel a sense of worry about the future. The rapid changes in how we consume media and the constant stream of information have heightened our sense of vulnerability. But while fear is a normal reaction, it doesn't have to control you. This book has offered practical steps to help transform that fear into productive action—preparation, awareness, and resilience. Remember, acknowledging your fear is the first step toward managing it effectively.

By simply reading this book and taking its guidance seriously, you've already demonstrated the foresight and strength needed to face whatever challenges may come. You are now equipped with the knowledge and mental resilience to weather storms that once felt overwhelming. The fact that you've made it this far is evidence of your ability to take control of your future, even in uncertain times.

Summarizing the Key Takeaways

1. Be Prepared, Not Paranoid

Throughout this book, we've emphasized a balanced approach to preparedness. The goal is not to live in fear or become obsessed with potential dangers, but to take reasonable, proactive steps to protect yourself and your family. Preparation gives you peace of mind. It means you're equipped to handle challenges before they arise, reducing the chaos and fear that often accompany emergencies.

Being prepared starts with having a plan. It means understanding the threats, whether it's civil unrest, natural disasters, or other crises, and then creating an actionable plan to face those threats. This includes everything from assembling go-bags, securing your home, establishing communication protocols, and knowing when to evacuate.

When you prepare calmly and rationally, you create a buffer between yourself and the panic that can grip society in times of crisis. That space allows you to make clearer decisions, protect your loved ones, and even help your neighbors. Remember, the goal is to be ready, not afraid.

Empowering Yourself Through Preparation

Staying prepared is about more than just stockpiling

supplies or having an evacuation plan. It's about cultivating the mindset that allows you to face unexpected challenges calmly and effectively. You've learned practical steps to protect your home, your family, and yourself in moments of crisis. Whether it's securing your home, managing health emergencies, or staying safe during an evacuation, you now have a foundation that allows you to act with confidence.

While preparation is key, it's also important to remain adaptable. The world is unpredictable, and no plan is ever perfect. Flexibility and the willingness to adjust your approach are essential for long-term resilience. When the world changes—whether through political shifts, social unrest, or environmental challenges—your ability to stay informed and adjust your plans will make the difference.

Remember, while you can't control everything, you can always control how prepared you are and how you respond. The world will continue to change, sometimes in unexpected ways, but adaptability is your greatest strength. Keep your plans flexible, remain informed, and always be ready to adjust to new situations.

2. Stay Calm, Stay Smart

Remaining calm in moments of chaos is a skill that can be developed with practice. Mental preparedness is just as important as physical readiness. Throughout the book, we've emphasized techniques like breathing exercises, breaking tasks into small, manageable steps, and staying focused on what you can control in the moment. These strategies help you stay grounded and rational when it matters most.

Being mentally calm not only protects you but also helps you serve as an anchor for others. During emergencies, people often look to those who are composed and collected for guidance. By remaining calm, you can help reduce the collective panic around you and contribute to a safer, more orderly response to the crisis.

3. Build Community Resilience

No one can survive alone, especially during prolonged periods of unrest. As we've discussed in previous chapters, communities that support each other are more likely to survive crises and recover faster. Building strong relationships with your neighbors, local groups, and trusted friends is crucial.

Community resilience means pooling resources, sharing information, and offering support when needed. This might mean forming neighborhood safety groups, checking in on vulnerable neighbors, or simply offering encouragement during difficult times. When we face challenges together, we are more likely to come out stronger and more united.

Communities that work together are not only better equipped to survive crises—they are also better able to rebuild. By fostering connections before, during, and after times of unrest, you help create a foundation of trust and collaboration that can last well beyond the immediate crisis.

4. Reassess and Adapt Your Plans

Preparedness is not a one-time effort. It requires regular reassessment and adaptation. Threats evolve, and so should your plans. Whether it's updating your go-bag, revising your evacuation routes, or adjusting your communication strategies, staying ready means being flexible and open to change.

As we discussed in Chapter 9, once the crisis subsides, it's important to reassess what worked and what didn't. Perhaps you discovered a weak point in your home security or realized that your communication plan needed improvement. Use these insights to make long-term improvements so that you are even more prepared the next time around.

The skills and strategies you've learned throughout this book are the foundation, but it's up to you to continue building on them. Stay curious, keep learning, and refine your plans as the world around you changes. The more you learn, the better prepared you'll be for the next challenge.

Helping others on this journey is another way to reinforce your own resilience. By sharing what you've learned with friends, family, or neighbors, you're not only helping them prepare but also contributing to a culture of readiness that benefits everyone. Preparedness is not a solo effort; it's something we all contribute to, and by doing so, we create a future where more people are ready to face the unknown.

Resilience is not just about getting through a crisis—it's about learning from it and becoming stronger as a result.

Final Thoughts on Maintaining Resilience in the Face of Uncertainty

Resilience Is a Lifelong Practice

Resilience isn't something you build once and forget about. It's a lifelong practice, just like physical fitness or learning. The challenges we face as individuals and communities may change over time, but the principles of resilience remain the same: staying calm, staying prepared, and working together.

In today's rapidly shifting world, maintaining resilience requires a mindset of continuous learning and growth. You must be willing to adapt to new circumstances, confront new threats, and stay engaged with your community. Resilience is not just about protecting yourself in times of crisis—it's about thriving in a world where change is constant.

Focus on Emotional and Mental Well-Being

Resilience is not only about physical preparedness—it's also about emotional and mental well-being. After any major crisis, processing the fear, grief, and trauma you've experienced is essential for healing and moving forward. In many ways, emotional resilience is what will allow you to bounce back stronger than before.

Taking the time to reflect on what happened, talking openly with family members—especially children—and reconnecting with your community are all important steps in the recovery process. It's okay to feel shaken after a crisis, but it's important to know that healing is possible.

There are several ways to build emotional and mental resilience:

- Talk about your experiences: Don't bottle up your feelings. Discuss the event with loved ones or even a counselor if necessary.

- Practice mindfulness: Techniques like meditation, journaling, or simply spending time in nature can help you process stress and trauma.

- Stay connected: Don't isolate yourself. Reaching out to your community or support networks can be incredibly healing.

- Focus on what you can control: In times of uncertainty, it's easy to feel overwhelmed by the "what ifs." Ground yourself by focusing on immediate actions you can take and what's within your control.

Moving Forward: Looking to the Future with Confidence

No one can predict the future with certainty. We don't know when the next crisis or period of unrest will arise, but that doesn't mean we are powerless. By preparing today, you are taking proactive steps to safeguard your future and your loved ones.

If there's one thing this guide hopes to impart, it's that you can face whatever comes next with confidence. Whether it's another round of civil unrest, a natural disaster, or an unexpected emergency, you now have the tools and mindset to navigate through it.

Remember, you are not alone. When we build resilience within ourselves and within our communities, we create a powerful network of strength that can weather any storm. While the future may be uncertain, your ability to respond to it doesn't have to be.

As you close this book, remember: preparation, mental resilience, and community are your strongest allies. You are not powerless in the face of uncertainty. You are capable, prepared, and ready to face whatever comes next. The steps you take today will protect you tomorrow. The strength you've developed throughout this book will carry you through whatever the future holds.

In the face of uncertainty, you now possess the tools to stay calm, make informed decisions, and act with purpose. Embrace that power, continue to grow, and always be ready to adapt. The world may be unpredictable, but you are prepared.

Case Study:
Rebuilding the United States After the Civil War

The American Civil War (1861-1865) was one of the darkest and most transformative periods in U.S. history. It tore the nation apart, claiming the lives of approximately 620,000 Americans and leaving deep scars that would take decades to heal. The war not only pitted North against South, but also left the country grappling with fundamental questions about freedom, equality, and the future of the nation. In the immediate aftermath, the U.S. faced the daunting challenge of reunification, rebuilding the Southern economy, and redefining the nation's identity. This case study explores how the U.S. attempted to recover from the war, the lingering issues that still resonate today, and the strides forward that were made in the years after the conflict.

The Immediate Aftermath: Reconstruction (1865-1877)

Reconstruction was the period following the Civil War during which the federal government attempted to reunify the fractured country, rebuild the South, and address the legal status of freed African Americans. The Reconstruction era was marked by political turmoil, social upheaval, and significant, though incomplete, progress in civil rights. This period laid the groundwork for some of the most consequential developments in American history, but also set the stage for long-standing issues that would persist for generations.

1. Rebuilding the South

The South, where most of the fighting took place, was left devastated. Its infrastructure—railroads, farms, and cities—was in ruins. Confederate currency was worthless, leaving many without the means to survive, and the economy, heavily reliant on slavery, had collapsed. Farmers who had relied on slave labor were now forced to adopt new methods of labor, often turning to sharecropping, which perpetuated economic inequality and debt for generations.

Key Challenges:

> **Economic Collapse**: The Southern economy, largely based on agriculture and the institution of slavery, was destroyed. Rebuilding it required not only physical reconstruction but also a new economic model, which was complicated by the widespread poverty and destruction.
>
> **Political Instability**: The question of how to reintegrate Southern states into the Union was hotly contested. Radical Republicans in Congress pushed for sweeping changes, including civil rights for freed slaves, while many Southerners resisted these efforts.

Major Strides:

- The Reconstruction Amendments: The 13th, 14th, and 15th Amendments were monumental in redefining American citizenship and expanding civil rights. The 13th Amendment (1865) abolished slavery, the 14th Amendment (1868) granted citizenship and equal protection under the law to all born in the U.S., and the 15th Amendment (1870) gave African American men the right to vote. These amendments were critical steps forward in American society, though their enforcement would remain inconsistent for many years.

2. Freedmen's Bureau and Education

The Freedmen's Bureau, established in 1865, was tasked with helping former slaves transition to freedom. This included providing food, housing, and medical aid, as well as establishing schools. Education was a critical area of progress during Reconstruction, as freed African Americans sought literacy and schooling in unprecedented numbers. The establishment of historically black colleges and universities (HBCUs), such as Howard University and Fisk University, began during this time and became vital institutions in the African American community.

Key Challenges:

Violent Backlash: The rise of white supremacist groups, such as the Ku Klux Klan, reflected the deep opposition to the integration of African Americans into the political and social fabric of the South. The Reconstruction governments faced significant violence and resistance, which undermined their efforts at reform.

Black Codes and Jim Crow: Despite the gains of Reconstruction, many Southern states enacted Black Codes aimed at restricting the rights and movements of freed African Americans. These laws laid the groundwork for the Jim Crow system of racial segregation that would dominate the South for nearly a century.

Major Strides:

- Educational Advances: While the South remained economically depressed, the post-war period saw a significant expansion in education for African Americans. By the end of Reconstruction, African American literacy rates had increased dramatically, sowing the seeds for future generations of black leadership and activism.

The Long-Term Challenges: *Lingering Effects of the Civil War*

Despite the end of slavery and the legislative gains of Reconstruction, the Civil War left deep and unresolved issues that continue to shape American society today.

1. Racial Inequality and Jim Crow

The end of Reconstruction in 1877, when federal troops were withdrawn from the South, marked the beginning of a long period of racial segregation and disenfranchisement. The rise of Jim Crow laws institutionalized racial discrimination in the South, undoing many of the gains made during Reconstruction. African Americans were systematically denied the right to vote, segregated in schools and public places, and subjected to lynchings and mob violence.

This period of racial inequality, which lasted well into the 20th century, is a direct legacy of the failure to fully address the racial divide created by the Civil War. Even after the civil rights movement of the 1960s, issues like systemic racism, police violence, and economic inequality still echo the deep divisions that the Civil War laid bare.

2. Economic Disparities

The Southern economy, devastated by the war and the loss of its labor force, took decades to recover.

Sharecropping and tenant farming became the norm, trapping many African Americans—and poor whites—in cycles of debt and poverty. The region remained largely agricultural and impoverished, in stark contrast to the industrial growth of the North. Even today, many Southern states struggle with higher levels of poverty, lower levels of education, and poorer health outcomes compared to the rest of the country.

Major Strides Forward: *Unity and Progress*

Despite the immense challenges, the post-Civil War period also saw the United States make remarkable strides toward becoming a more unified and equitable society.

1. Civil Rights and the Long Arc of Justice

While it took nearly a century after the Civil War to dismantle Jim Crow, the war and Reconstruction set the foundation for the civil rights movement of the 1950s and 1960s. The fight for equality, led by figures like Martin Luther King Jr., Rosa Parks, and Malcolm X, was built on the legal and moral precedents established during Reconstruction. The civil rights movement culminated in landmark legislation like the Civil Rights Act of 1964 and the Voting Rights Act of 1965, which finally addressed many of the racial injustices that had lingered since the end of the Civil War.

2. Economic and Industrial Expansion

While the South struggled, the North experienced a period of rapid industrial growth after the Civil War, helping to transform the United States into a global economic power. The war had spurred innovations in manufacturing, transportation (particularly the railroad system), and communication. This laid the groundwork for the Gilded Age, during which the U.S. became an industrial powerhouse, attracting immigrants from around the world and building the modern economy.

3. National Identity and Reconciliation

Though the post-war years were fraught with tension, the U.S. gradually found ways to reconcile its divisions. Memorials and national holidays like Memorial Day emerged to honor soldiers from both sides of the conflict, helping to heal the wounds of war. By the early 20th century, veterans of the Civil War—Union and Confederate—gathered at joint reunions, a symbol of the nation's effort to reunite and move forward together.

Conclusion: The Long Journey Toward Unity

The recovery from the Civil War was neither quick nor easy. It took decades of struggle, compromise, and conflict to rebuild the nation. Many of the divisions and inequities that were born out of the war still linger in American society today, as seen in ongoing racial tensions, economic disparities, and debates about the legacy of the Confederacy. However, the strides made in civil rights, the rise of the U.S. as an industrial power, and the resilience of the American people in rebuilding their communities are lasting testaments to the nation's capacity for unity and progress.

The Civil War fundamentally reshaped the United States, and its lessons continue to influence the country's political and social landscape. While the scars of the war remain, the journey toward a more just and equitable society continues, built on the foundations laid in the years following the conflict.

Lessons to Be Learned

In the event of a major civil unrest in the future, we must learn from the past on how to come together stronger once the storm has passed. The recovery and reunification process after the Civil War provides many valuable lessons for addressing major civil unrest caused by deep political rifts, such as those that could arise from a future election. These lessons revolve around the importance of reconciliation, addressing underlying causes of division, and building institutions and systems that promote unity and long-term stability. Here are some key takeaways that can be applied to future unrest:

1. Address Underlying Grievances Head-On

One of the most critical lessons from the Civil War and Reconstruction is that superficial peace without addressing underlying grievances only leads to prolonged tension. After the war, the failure to fully address racial inequality, voting rights, and economic disparities, especially in the South, led to the rise of Jim Crow laws, systemic racism, and segregation that lasted for nearly a century. Similarly, if future civil unrest is caused by political divisions, it's essential to address the root causes of those divisions rather than merely seeking a temporary end to the conflict.

Application: If a future political rift leads to unrest, the solution must go beyond calling for calm. Political leaders must address the reasons for the unrest—whether it's economic inequality, political disenfranchisement, or cultural grievances. This means working to create electoral reforms, addressing misinformation, ensuring fair voting access, & fostering economic policies that include all citizens.

2. Reconciliation Must Be Proactive and Genuine

In the years after the Civil War, the federal government attempted to foster reconciliation through Reconstruction policies and the reintegration of Southern states into the Union. However, a genuine sense of national unity was slow to develop, and many white Southerners resisted Reconstruction's goals, eventually resulting in the rise of segregation and institutional racism. The lesson here is that reconciliation must be both proactive and sustained over time. Attempts to force reconciliation without meaningful dialogue or mutual understanding are likely to fail.

Application: After any major civil unrest, especially one based on political divides, genuine efforts toward reconciliation must involve listening to both sides, fostering open dialogue, and addressing legitimate concerns from all groups. Leaders from both sides of the political spectrum must engage in constructive conversations, showing respect for differing perspectives while firmly opposing violent, discriminatory or extremist behaviors.

3. Rebuild Institutions That Can Foster Unity

One of the challenges after the Civil War was rebuilding institutions that could support national unity. Although the Union was preserved, many Southern institutions (education, law enforcement, local governments) retained discriminatory policies, which perpetuated division. One of the successes, however, was the establishment of new public institutions, such as historically Black colleges and universities (HBCUs), which provided education and opportunities to African Americans, helping them build social capital and a sense of belonging.

Application: In the wake of major unrest, it's crucial to invest in rebuilding & reforming institutions—particularly those tied to governance, education, and the legal system—that can foster greater inclusivity and civic participation. Public institutions, electoral bodies, the media, & community organizations must be reoriented toward transparency, fairness, and the active inclusion of all groups, regardless of political affiliation. Ensuring that these institutions are trustworthy can rebuild public confidence & promote stability.

4. Economic Reconstruction Should Be Inclusive

After the Civil War, the Southern economy was devastated, and many attempts at rebuilding did not fully include African Americans or poor white citizens in the process. The sharecropping system that emerged often kept former slaves in cycles of debt, and land reforms were largely abandoned, exacerbating economic inequality. Long-term economic recovery should be focused on inclusion and providing opportunities for all, especially those who were marginalized during the unrest.

Application: In the aftermath of future civil unrest, ensuring economic recovery is equitable and inclusive will be crucial for preventing future unrest. Policies should aim at closing wealth gaps, increasing access to education, creating jobs, and ensuring that marginalized communities—who may feel left behind by economic progress—are given a fair chance to thrive. Stimulus packages, infrastructure investment, and job programs that serve economically distressed areas can reduce the risk of future political or social instability.

5. Protect Civil Rights and Promote Legal Accountability

One of the enduring lessons from Reconstruction is the importance of protecting civil rights through legal frameworks, but also the danger of allowing those protections to erode. The Reconstruction Amendments (13th, 14th, and 15th Amendments) were a monumental step forward, yet their enforcement was inconsistent, and many of the legal protections for African Americans were undermined by local governments and courts.

Application: After any period of political or civil unrest, it's important to ensure that civil rights and the rule of law are strengthened. Legal reforms aimed at protecting voting rights, preventing political violence, and curbing disinformation must be enacted and upheld. Furthermore, those responsible for inciting violence or undermining democratic institutions must be held accountable, but in a way that prioritizes justice over vengeance. Fair legal processes can help prevent future unrest by signaling that no group is above the law.

6. Use Civic Education to Rebuild National Identity

After the Civil War, public education became a key way to instill values of national unity, particularly in the North. However, in the South, Lost Cause mythology and revisionist histories became dominant in schools, which glorified the Confederacy and justified segregation. This division in historical memory contributed to lingering tensions and misunderstandings.

Application: In the wake of future unrest, national unity can be fostered through civic education. This means creating education systems that teach a fair and balanced history, emphasizing democratic values, the importance of civil rights, and the dangers of political extremism. Fostering a shared understanding of history and the country's founding principles can help reduce polarization in future generations.

7. Community Support and Rebuilding Trust

After the Civil War, community ties were crucial in the South and North alike for rebuilding trust among citizens. Though it took many years, rebuilding efforts were often driven by communities coming together to support one another, whether through rebuilding infrastructure, establishing local economies, or creating new forms of local governance. However, mistrust between different racial and political groups often remained, which hindered reconciliation.

Application: Community support networks are essential

after a major crisis or unrest. Encouraging grassroots efforts where neighbors help neighbors can rebuild the bonds of trust that are often frayed during political crises. Programs that encourage collaboration—such as shared rebuilding projects, local initiatives for economic recovery, or neighborhood councils—can foster resilience and reduce the potential for future conflicts.

8. Long-Term Commitment to Healing

The aftermath of the Civil War shows us that healing from deep national divisions takes time—sometimes decades or more. Reconstruction officially ended in 1877, but the issues of racial inequality and division persisted into the 20th century, and many still remain today. However, the progress made over the last 150 years—from civil rights legislation to economic expansion—shows that, over time, a country can heal from even the most bitter conflicts.

Application: Future unrest caused by political divides will also require a long-term commitment to healing. There is no quick fix. Political leaders, community organizations, and citizens must be prepared for a sustained effort to bridge divides, rebuild trust, and create systems that prevent similar unrest in the future. This could involve sustained dialogues, reforms to political systems, and policies that prioritize inclusion and fairness.

Learning from the Past

The U.S. recovery after the Civil War offers both cautionary and hopeful lessons for how to handle future unrest caused by deep political divides. The war demonstrated the catastrophic consequences of division, but it also showed the potential for a country to rebuild and progress if it commits to reconciliation, inclusivity, and justice. In the event of future political unrest, the U.S.

must focus on healing rifts, ensuring fair governance, and creating economic and social systems that allow all citizens to thrive. While the scars of unrest may take years to heal, history shows that sustained commitment can lead to a stronger, more unified society.

ABOUT THE AUTHOR

Barrett Cole is a seasoned intelligence and force protection officer with over a decade of experience in analyzing and managing global crisis situations. He has operated in more than a dozen countries, often in regions facing significant political instability and civil unrest. Having served multiple combat deployments and traveled extensively to areas impacted by conflict, Barrett brings firsthand experience in navigating high-risk environments. His expertise in crisis preparedness, including time spent in countries on the brink of revolution like Sudan in 2019, offers readers practical, actionable strategies to stay safe and resilient in uncertain times.